ARCHITECTS
In Albany

ARCHITECTS
In Albany

Edited by Diana S. Waite

MOUNT IDA PRESS

HISTORIC ALBANY FOUNDATION

MOUNT IDA PRESS

111 Washington Avenue
Albany, NY 12210
518.426.5935
www.mountidapress.com

HISTORIC ALBANY FOUNDATION

89 Lexington Avenue
Albany, NY 12206
518.465.0876
www.historic-albany.org

Published 2009. Printed in the United States of America.
Design: The Market Street Group www.marketstreetgroup.com
Printing: Thomson-Shore www.tshore.com

Funding for this book was generously provided by The Bender Family Foundation, Matthew Bender IV, Furthermore: a program of the J. M. Kaplan Fund, and a Campus Heritage Grant from the Getty Foundation in Los Angeles to the University at Albany Foundation, SUNY.

ISBN: 978-0-9625368-6-1

Library of Congress Cataloging-in-Publication Data

Architects in Albany / edited by Diana S. Waite. — 2nd ed.
    p. cm.
  Rev. ed. of: Albany architects : the present looks at the past. 1978.
  Includes index.
  ISBN 978-0-9625368-6-1
  1. Architects—New York (State)—Albany—Biography.
  2. Architecture—New York (State)—Albany. 3. Albany (N.Y.)—Buildings, structures, etc. I. Waite, Diana S. II. Albany architects.
   NA735.A39A73 2010
   720.92′274743—dc22
                                    2009034899

Front cover photograph credits
Portraits, clockwise from top left: Albert W. Fuller, Fort Orange Club archives. Ethan A. Dennison, courtesy of Mrs. E. Allen Dennison Jr. Walter H. Van Guysling, courtesy of Mark H. Van Guysling. Isaac Perry with his granddaughter Lucretia Perry, courtesy of New York State Commission on the Restoration of the Capitol (hereafter, NYSCRC). Henry Hobson Richardson, courtesy of NYSCRC. Buildings, clockwise from top left: Great Western Staircase, New York State Capitol, courtesy of NYSCRC. St. Peter's Episcopal Church, Truck House No. 4, Home Savings Bank, Gov. Nelson A. Rockefeller Empire State Plaza, courtesy of M. McCarty and G. Gold.

Back cover photograph credits
Portraits, left to right: Henry L. Blatner, courtesy of Mary Blatner Valentis, PhD. Leopold Eidlitz, courtesy of NYSCRC. Marcus T. Reynolds, c. 1897, Fort Orange Club Archives, MG 186, Albany Institute of History & Art. Robert W. Gibson, courtesy of Stephen Van C. Wilberding. Buildings: Delaware and Hudson Building and Albany Evening Journal Building (left), courtesy of M. McCarty and G. Gold. State Library Reading Room, New York State Education Building, courtesy of New York State Library.

Contents

Editor's Note and Acknowledgments

The idea for this publication originated late in 2004, when Matthew Bender IV proposed that a 24-year-old booklet entitled *Albany Architects* be updated and expanded. That slender volume was still a very popular reference work but had long been out of print. The new book would triple the number of essays on architects and their firms, and it would offer the opportunity to focus on notable designers of the mid-twentieth century. The new book, entitled *Architects in Albany,* would be a collaborative project of the original publisher, Historic Albany Foundation, and of Mount Ida Press.

Creating the new book proved to be a major project involving many people in the creation of the content. The surviving authors of the original essays were invited to update their materials. The candidate architects for the new essays were winnowed down from scores of prospects, and to afford some historical perspective, it was agreed not to include living architects. Cornelia Brooke Gilder, who had edited the original book, agreed to write 16 of the new profiles, and other experts were engaged to produce the remaining 8. Matthew Bender and Susan Holland, the executive director of Historic Albany Foundation, were our excellent partners throughout the project.

Over the years many people contributed important historical research and editorial suggestions, including William Brandow, Frederick D. Cawley, Elizabeth Doviak, Colonie town historian Kevin Franklin, E. J. Johnson, Jessica Fisher Neidl, Kevin O'Connor of Siena College, Albany city historian Tony Opalka, Paul R. Huey, Roger G. Reed, Norman S. Rice, Walter Richard Wheeler, Geoffrey Williams and Brian Keough of the Department of Special Collections and Archives at the University at Albany, and Christiana Limniatis and Cara R. Macri of Historic Albany Foundation.

The illustrations from the original book had been lost, so replacements were located and more pictures gathered for the new essays. Gary David Gold and Mark McCarty very graciously permitted the use of many photographs that had been commissioned for *Albany Architecture: A Guide to the City.* Tammis Groft, her staff, and volunteers at the Albany Institute of History & Art Library generously accommodated the search for illustrations: former chief librarian and archivist Rebecca Rich-Wulfmeyer, Phoebe Powell Bender, Barbara Bertucio, Barbara Casey, Janine Moon, Allison Munsell, Tom Nelson, and Jackaline Ring. Paul Mercer and the staff of the Manuscripts and Special Collections Division of the New York State Library and James Hobin at the Albany Public Library helped locate additional images. William Brandow, Douglas G. Bucher, Norman Rice, Jeanne Stephens, and Mark Van Guysling shared illustrations from their personal collections. Joe Putrock contributed several new photographs.

The University at Albany, State University of New York, assisted from the beginning years of the project. William B. Hedberg, Associate Vice President for Academic Affairs, provided important institutional support, and Professor Mary Blatner Valentis, PhD, was an important advocate of the book. Librarian Carol Lee Anderson, assisted by Euni Chang, oversaw the conversion of the original text to electronic files.

At Mount Ida Press Melissa Miščević Bramble, Maya E. Rook, and Jessica Fisher Neidl played important roles with the detailed research and editorial work needed to turn the manuscript into a book. Interns Meghan Dunn, Kristy Kolb, Meaghan Polson, and Alexandra Preuss assisted the Mount Ida Press staff. Constance Timm of the Market Street Group provided the graphic design, carefully integrating the varied images with the text.

As the work drew to a close, Matthew Bender, William Brandow, Douglas Bucher, Susan Holland, Jack McEneny, and Norman Rice carefully read the final manuscript, offering suggestions and correcting errors. Nevertheless, despite the countless hours spent by the staff of Mount Ida Press and the help of the readers, there are so many details and facts in a book of this nature that inevitably some mistakes and inconsistencies still remain. Please let us know about them so that they can be corrected in the next printing.

This book would never have appeared in print without the substantial underwriting provided by The Bender Family Foundation, Matthew Bender IV, and Furthermore: a program of the J. M. Kaplan Fund. The book was also made possible with the generous support of a Campus Heritage Grant from the Getty Foundation in Los Angeles to the University at Albany Foundation, SUNY.

There are many other accomplished architects whose handsome works line the streets of Albany. Hopefully this volume will not only foster additional investigation into the work of the architects who are profiled here but also spur new research about architects who were not included.

Diana S. Waite
President
Mount Ida Press
August 2009

Introduction to the Second Edition, 2009

Thirty-one years ago, in 1978, Historic Albany Foundation published *Albany Architects: The Present Looks at the Past*, a booklet featuring 12 well-known architects and architectural firms that had made their imprint on the city. Historic Albany Foundation, established in 1974, was still in its infancy when the book was published. Historic Albany's founders had started the organization with a cause celebre but also with a vision of educating the public about Albany's architectural heritage.

The cause celebre was to preserve and revitalize what was left of the mid- to late-nineteenth-century architecture in the Center Square and Hudson/Park neighborhoods once the South Mall was completed. Now known as the Empire State Plaza, the South Mall was built between 1962 and 1978 at Governor Nelson A. Rockefeller's direction; it destroyed 1,500 historic buildings and displaced some 7,000 residents. To help fulfill its additional mission of documenting Albany's historic buildings and educating the public about them, Historic Albany Foundation's staff and board of directors embarked on a small but ambitious publication about the city's architects and their work.

This new edition of that book, retitled *Architects in Albany*, continues to celebrate and promote Albany's nineteenth- and twentieth-century buildings, including those that are only 50 years old. The public is familiar with many of these buildings but might not know their designers; the hope is that this book will dispel myths and bring to life the many nationally known and local architects who left an indelible mark on the city. Included are updated biographies for the original 12 entries, as well as 24 new profiles, along with extensive lists of the architects' works in Albany. The illustrations have been expanded as well.

Many of the buildings featured here, both grand and not so grand, were demolished years ago, some in the name of "progress," some to make room for finer buildings erected in their place, as with the U.S. Post Office and Courthouse by Gander, Gander and Gander or the Delaware and Hudson and Albany Evening Journal buildings by Marcus T. Reynolds. Other demolished buildings, though, were not replaced by better buildings. Looking forward, when new construction is called for, it is hoped that architects of local and national repute will build excellent new buildings to match the quality of Albany's fine historic structures. A look back in 30 years will determine what will be worthy to include in a new publication like this one.

For now, one can be content to peruse this fine collection of the best late eighteenth-, nineteenth-, and twentieth-century buildings. There is a lot to celebrate, digest, and absorb in regard to the early and later architects who gave the city of Albany an awe-inspiring collection of buildings.

Susan Herlands Holland
Executive Director
Historic Albany Foundation
August 2009

Introduction to the First Edition, 1978
Albany Architects: Yesterday Versus Today

The yellow pages list better than six dozen architects practicing in the Albany area today. Yet one looks nearly in vain for memorable evidence of their handiwork. Can this paucity of noteworthy contemporary architecture in our city be attributed to the economic slump of the region or to the growth of suburbs and carpetbagging activity from New York City firms, or does it merely reflect the inability of the current crop of local practitioners to produce artistically significant buildings? No doubt each of these explanations has contributed, but I suspect the real reason is that architecture in Albany is overwhelmingly an affair of the nineteenth century and that nineteenth-century architects have indelibly shaped the face of the city.

At every turn we are confronted with the nineteenth century—homes, public buildings, streets, parks; indeed, the spirit of that age is so pervasive that modern buildings tend to be misfits, and even vacant lots speak more strongly of loss than promise for the future.

We live in the wake of recent efforts to rebuild Albany, efforts which in retrospect may be seen as acts of devastation nearly as brutal as the World War II destruction of European cities. Union Station is in ruins; the Albany Savings Bank is no more; the Pruyn Library succumbed to a sprawling highway system; Keeler's Restaurant is scattered in fragments; Van Heusen & Charles has given way to bankers' cars; the Ten Eyck Hotel, Farnham's, Whitney's—gone, gone, gone. These landmarks and more combined to make Albany the unique place we knew. That place was victim of forces and attitudes we did not fully comprehend nor know how to cope with at the time. Now, like the post-war citizens of Warsaw and Würzburg, we want our old city back.

The lost landmarks cannot be retrieved. In publishing these essays, however, Historic Albany is regaining the past for us, illuminating familiar names and others nearly forgotten, and compiling architectural credits that help sift fact from fiction. Together these essays are the first step in providing a better understanding of the visible city which architects have created here over the course of the past 150 years. For the architectural historian fallow ground at last is being worked; for the laymen new associations, names, and dates can be ascribed to familiar landmarks; for the practicing architect the realization should take root that in his work nothing fundamental changes. Even the problems are the same: inadequate budgets, unimaginative building committees, indifferent workmen, impatient clients and always the nagging doubt that something better could have been done, if only. . .

In the end the challenge for an architect remains always the same: to create within the world as it is—usually indifferent, sometimes hostile, never ideal—a world as he would have it. In this sense, architects of the 1970s, 1870s, or 1770s share a common bond. Each in a small way, building by building, changes the earth. Like a forester who plants a field of saplings that in time becomes a sheltering forest, a gifted builder of buildings leaves behind him a reality which would not exist, but for his coming. And, when generation after generation of architects touches the same city, a remarkable layering of the human presence is achieved that makes the city unforgettable.

These realizations should engender new attitudes. First, renewal of the city does not require the destruction of the old. Existing structures themselves can be renewed, thereby saving the familiar while accommodating new needs. Second, we should approach the surviving work of our predecessors with respect—perhaps even reverence—and temper our own estimate of our abilities with considerable modesty. When we touch old buildings, whether to restore or to renovate, we must first study them thoroughly, understand the original architect's intentions, and above all refrain from willfully subjecting them to current design whims or expedient modernization techniques. Third, when we seek to alter the fabric of the city, whether by constructing highways and plazas or filling the vacant lots with new buildings, we must appreciate the texture and character of the space in which we build as it has evolved over the centuries. In these endeavors historians, architects, developers, and laymen each have responsibilities, which, when joined in a common purpose, can create once again an Albany wherein old and new exist in mutual harmony.

John I Mesick
Partner
Mendel, Mesick and Cohen

Philip Hooker

Douglas G. Bucher

Philip Hooker (1766–1836) was involved in projects throughout upstate New York, including Albany, Troy, Rensselaer, Schenectady, and Utica. In Albany, however, he completely dominated the architectural scene beginning in 1797. By 1830 virtually every important public building in the city had been designed by Hooker, including the state Capitol (1804–1809), the jail (1810), Albany Academy (1815), city hall (1829), and the Clinton and Washington markets (1829). The spires of Hooker's many churches ornamented the city's skyline. His first documented work was the twin-spired North Dutch Reformed Church, begun in 1797 and, remarkably, still extant.

Born in the town of Rutland, Massachusetts, on October 28, 1766, Hooker moved to Albany with his parents, Samuel and Rachel Hooker, around 1772. The family included five sons and two daughters. As a young man Philip worked with his father, who was a carpenter-builder.

Nothing is known about Philip Hooker's education or other early experience. His involvement in building can be dated to about 1790 by a statement he made in 1815 that he had "an experience of twenty-five years in building and a close application in the research of antient and modern architecture." He may have spent some time in New York City, where the city directories for 1792 and 1793 included a Philip Hooker who was a house carpenter.

In 1793 the French émigré architect-engineers Pierre Pharoux and Simon Desjardins arrived in Albany, and these experienced designers likely influenced the young Hooker. Stylistically, he also may have been influenced by the works of Charles Bulfinch, of Boston, and John McComb, of New York City, and by the pattern books of Asher Benjamin. Hooker likely assembled a personal library on architecture and engineering, and he certainly had access to the libraries of his wealthy clients. It is known that he owned a copy of Abraham Swan's *The Carpenters Complete Instructor, in Several Hundred Designs* (London, 1768), for a copy now in a private collection is inscribed on the flyleaf with his name and the date 1797. In the same year Hooker's parents and siblings moved from Albany to Utica, New York.

The Albany Academy (1815–1816) in Academy Park, the North Dutch Reformed Church (1797–1799), Hyde Hall (1817–1835) near Cooperstown, and the Hamilton College Chapel (1825–1827) are Hooker's finest surviving buildings. The architectural detailing of the Albany Academy may have been influenced by McComb's city hall in New York City (1803–1812) and is French rather than English in derivation. The bold carving in the interior is characteristic of Hooker and of the craftsman he favored,

Albany Academy, east facade, Academy Park. Courtesy of the author.

particularly woodcarver Henry Farnham. The former chapel on the second floor of the Academy, one of the great public rooms of its period in the U.S., has survived remarkably intact. The Academy building is now used as offices by the Albany City School District.

Hooker's design for the facade of the New York State National Bank (1803) on lower State Street was certainly

Albany City Hall, Eagle Street. Courtesy of the author.

Albany Academy. Courtesy of the author.

inspired by the design for the Society for the Encouragement of Arts, Manufactures and Commerce by Robert and James Adam in London. Rondelles on the London facade feature classical figures, but for Albany Hooker used oversized representations of the obverse and reverse of an 1803 silver dollar. Hooker's facade was carefully preserved by architect Henry Ives Cobb, who had the facade moved several feet up State Street to become the central feature of his multi-story New York State National Bank building of 1927.

Although Hooker designed many elegant residences, little of his domestic work survives today in Albany. With his father, he remodeled the house of the New York secretary of state (1806), enlarged the Van Rensselaer Manor House (1818), and designed new houses for such wealthy citizens as Peter Gansevoort (circa 1815), Elsie Fonda (1802), Samuel Hill (1812), Josephus Bradner Stuart (1818), and Stephen Van Rensselaer IV (1817). Prospect, the Arbor Hill house built for Abraham and Elizabeth Van Rensselaer Ten Broeck (1797), may be his earliest domestic work. In 1817 Hooker and George Clarke began a long professional relationship that would result in the great country house known as Hyde Hall (1817–1835) on Lake Otsego.

Hooker's work also included such utilitarian buildings as warehouses for Henry Van Schaick and John Holme (1827) and a mortuary vault for the Van Rensselaer family (1823). He also designed a number of iron fences and stoop rails for public and private clients in the city. He was a versatile architect involved in all aspects of the profession, including the acquisition of materials and supervision of construction, probably the result of the early training received from his father.

Hooker was very active in public life, to the benefit of his architectural practice. As assessor for the fourth ward, alderman, city superintendent, and city surveyor, he was in the forefront of the city's development at a critical period. He was also a founder of the Mechanics' Society of Albany (1801) and a member of the Fine Arts Committee of the Society for the Promotion of Useful Arts.

Albany was Hooker's home for 64 years. He married twice and in later years frequently changed his address. He died on January 21, 1836, at 130 Green Street, a simple, two-story brick house that was part of a row of six identical townhouses that Hooker may have designed for William James about 1826.

Henry Rector

Norman S. Rice and Walter Richard Wheeler

Henry Rector was born on November 4, 1793, in Duanesburg, New York, a descendant of Palatine German immigrants. Rector moved to Albany by 1813 and married Jane Anne Sickles when he was 22. Their son William would later work in partnership with his father. Rector married again at least once; his final marriage was to Elizabeth Bowlsby, who also predeceased him.

Early in his career, from 1820 to 1827, Rector is listed in the city directories with various occupations, including carpenter, carpenter and grocer, carver, and builder. From 1824 until 1829 he worked in Albany in partnership with Darius Geer, brother of the well-known New York City builder Seth Geer. In 1829 Rector was not listed in the Albany directories; he may have spent some time in the circle of architects Ithiel Town and Alexander Jackson Davis in New York City. The 1830 Albany directory is the first time the designation "architect" appears next to Rector's name.

Rector appears to have been a principal, if not the primary, successor to Philip Hooker. Hooker and Rector are the only two architects listed in the 1834 city directory. Their careers converged in the 1829 competition for the design of the Albany City Hall, which would become Hooker's last major Albany work. Thereafter it was an Albany field day for the younger architect. Hooker's protégés Robert Higham and James T. Kelly both became civil engineers specializing in railroads, so Rector remained the only practicing architect in the city during the second half of the 1830s.

Four of Rector's major buildings of the early 1830s—the Pearl Street Baptist Church, the Albany Female Academy, the Columbia County Courthouse in Hudson, and the State Hall (now the New York State Court of Appeals)—were designed in the Greek temple form with Ionic porticos having six columns. Also in the Greek Revival style, Rector's imposing Exchange building (1836) had massive, two-story Greek portals; located at the foot of State Street, it was the largest Albany office building of its day. Rector enjoyed professional prominence during the 1830s: he presented public lectures on architectural history, fielded commissions in distant locales, served as a professional witness, and was elected to public offices.

Rector's promising career was negatively impacted by his involvement in a lawsuit over his fees for designing the State Hall, which remained unsettled for more than ten years. That suit, together with his brother Thomas's trial

Pearl Street Baptist Church, North Pearl Street, east of State Street. Albany Institute of History & Art Library.

for murder in 1839, placed Rector's career under a cloud from which it never fully recovered. Prominent public commissions remained out of the question, and his work was largely relegated to the design of utilitarian structures for the City of Albany, such as firehouses and schools, and its merchants.

It was only in the late 1840s that Rector regained some of the professional prominence that he had enjoyed early on. With commissions such as the rectory for St. Peter's Church (1846–1847) and the First Presbyterian Church (1847–1850), Rector turned toward the Gothic

Revival style. By the 1850s, however, Albany had become the focus of practice for other architects, such as William L. Woollett, George I. Penchard, and John D. Towle, and Albany clients also engaged architects based in New York City.

From the mid-1850s until 1865 Rector was listed in city directories as living at 83 Hudson Avenue, a residence that also served for a time as an office; from then on until 1871 he moved from one boardinghouse to another. By June 1872 he had relocated to New York City, living out his days in the home of a niece, Josephine Curtis. He died in 1878 and was buried in the Albany Rural Cemetery, at his request.

Although only the State Hall and a row of speculative houses on Westerlo Street by Rector survive in Albany, there is little doubt that during his lifetime he contributed significantly to the physical development and enhancement of the city.

Albany Exchange, corner of Broadway and State Street. New York State Library.

Building List

1827–1828   Five speculative houses for Edward C. Delavan, N. Pearl St., north of Maiden La., partially demolished
1827–1828   Speculative houses for Edward C. Delavan, Chapel St., north of Maiden La., demolished
1828–1829   52–58 Westerlo St. (with Darius Geer)
1829   Competition entry for the Albany City Hall, not built
1830–1831   Bloodgood Stores, cor. of State St. and Dean St., demolished
1831   First Presbyterian Church, additions and renovations, S. Pearl St. bet. Norton St. and Beaver St., demolished
1831   Schoolhouse, Orchard St., demolished
1832   Albany Orphan Asylum, cor. of Western Ave. and Robin St., demolished

1832   Fence and gates, Capitol Park, demolished
1832–1834   Mount Hope (Ezra Prentice house), S. Pearl St., demolished
1832–1835   Stanwix Hall, SE cor. of Broadway and Maiden La., demolished
1833   Fence, Albany City Hall, demolished
1833   Gates, Academy Park, demolished
1833   State Hall (first design), not built
1833–1834   Albany Female Academy, N. Pearl St. bet. State St. and Maiden La., demolished
1833–1834   Pearl St. Baptist Church, N. Pearl St., east of State St., demolished
1835   Consistory room and dwelling, First Lutheran Church, Lodge St., not built
1835   Engine Company No. 4, Madison Ave., demolished
1835   Engine house, Chapel St., demolished
1835–1836   Schoolhouse and Engine Company No. 7, Hudson Ave., demolished
1835–1837   Third Reformed Protestant Dutch Church, NE cor. of S. Ferry St. and Green St., burned 1841, demolished
1835–1842   State Hall (now New York State Court of Appeals), Eagle St. bet. Pine St. and Columbia St., enlarged 1916 and 2005, refaced 1958–1959
1836   House for Martha Bradstreet, Albany area, probably not built
1836–1837   Albany Exchange, NE cor. of Broadway and State St., demolished
1837   Speculative row houses for First Lutheran Church, Capitol St., demolished
1837   Stores for C. L. Townsend estate (with William Rector), Broadway, demolished
1837   Stores for Gerrit Peebles and John Holme, remodeling, cor. of Dean St. and Exchange St., demolished
1839–1840   Pearl Street Theatre, conversion for use as St. Paul's Church, S. Pearl St., demolished
1841   Douw's buildings, SW cor. of Broadway and State St., demolished
1844   Consistory house, Middle Dutch Church, Beaver St., demolished
1844   Hudson Avenue Methodist Church (with William Rector), Hudson Ave. bet. Grand St. and Philip St., demolished
1844   State Street Baptist Church, cor. of State St. and High St., demolished
1846–1847   Rectory, St. Peter's Church, Lodge St., demolished
1847–1850   First Presbyterian Church (third building), cor. of Philip St. and Hudson Ave., demolished
1848–1849   Schoolhouse, Second St., demolished
1848–1849   Stores for John Marvin, Broadway, south of Trotter's Alley, demolished

James Renwick Jr.

Cornelia Brooke Gilder

An ascendant, young ecclesiastical architect from New York City, James Renwick Jr. (1818–1895), traveled to Albany three times between 1847 and 1849 to supervise the construction of Trinity Episcopal Church in the South End.

His first major work, the soaring stone Gothic Grace Church on Broadway and Tenth Street in New York City, was completed in 1846. Renwick was finishing the brownstone Calvary Church on Park Avenue and Twenty-First Street the year he was hired to design Trinity in Albany. Under the initiative of the Rev. Edward Selkirk, Trinity's building committee sought out young Renwick. On August 3, 1847, committee members traveled to New York City to interview him and see his churches. Working with a more modest budget at Trinity, Renwick offered the Albany congregation a simplified version of his Calvary Church—a cruciform plan, two towers with steeply pitched gables and crocketted pinnacles, and a large lancet window over the central door, one of a trio of Gothic portals. Four years later Renwick favored round arches and a single tower for the small-scale Dutch Reformed Church in Saugerties, but he continued to work in the Gothic Revival style for his masterpiece, St. Patrick's Cathedral on Fifth Avenue in New York City (1858–1879).

Renwick's mother, Margaret Brevoort, was a member of one of Manhattan's old Dutch landowning families, and his father was a leading engineer and a professor at Columbia College, where James studied. His first employment, in the mid-1830s, was as an engineer on the Erie Railroad and the Croton Reservoir in midtown Manhattan. Two of Renwick's brothers became engineers, and other family members were gifted artists and architects.

James Renwick's marriage to shipping heiress Anna Lloyd Aspinwall in 1851 might have allowed him an early retirement as a gentleman architect, but instead he continued for 40 more years, producing a wide array of stylistically varied and imaginative designs for public buildings, commercial structures, and private houses. The majority of these were constructed in the environs of New York City, but three notable exceptions are the Norman-style Smithsonian Institution (1847–1855), the Second Empire-style Corcoran Gallery (renamed the Renwick Gallery) in Washington, D.C. (1859–1871), and the Main Building at Vassar College in Poughkeepsie (1861–1865).

Over the years Renwick worked with a succession of partners: Richard T. Auchmuty in the late 1850s, Joseph Sands in the 1860s and 1870s, and his wife's cousin James L. Aspinwall and a nephew, William W. Renwick, in the 1880s and 1890s. Over six feet tall, commanding, and sometimes hot tempered, James Renwick was known affectionately to his juniors in the office in later years as "the old gentleman."

Standing on Trinity Place, a side street off Madison Avenue in the South End, Trinity Church, Albany's only Renwick-designed building, is forgotten and derelict. Long ago shorn of its decorative wooden tower gables and pinnacles, it still ranks as the city's second-oldest surviving Gothic structure.

Building List

1847–1849   Trinity Church, Trinity Pl. bet. Ash Grove Pl. and Madison Ave.

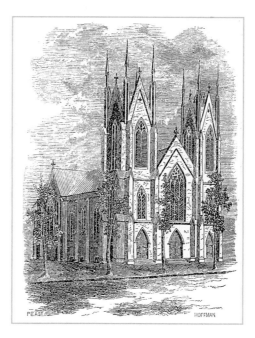

Trinity Church, Trinity Place between Ash Grove Place and Madison Avenue. Joel Munsell, Munsell's Annals of Albany, *vol. 3 (Albany: 1850). Albany Institute of History & Art Library.*

The Woolletts

Cornelia Brooke Gilder and Walter Richard Wheeler

During the second half of the nineteenth century three successive generations of the Woollett family practiced architecture in Albany. The English-born William Lee Woollett Jr. (1815–1874) handed on his practice to his son William M. Woollett (1850–1880). This second William died at the age of 30, but two of his children, William Lee and John, grew up to become architects and worked in Albany before moving to California early in the twentieth century.

The Woollett family had emigrated from Kent, England, to Philadelphia by 1819. William Lee Woollett Sr. (d. 1860) was the grandson of an internationally famous engraver, also named William (1735–1785), and worked as an engraver and portrait artist into the 1830s in the Philadelphia vicinity. The first of the trio of Albany architects was his son, William L. Woollett Jr., who was born in Wateringbury, near Maidstone, Kent, in 1815, but grew up in the Philadelphia area and apparently studied

architecture there. By 1840 he and his family had moved to Sand Lake in Rensselaer County.

The earliest mention of William L. Woollett Jr. as an architect appears in the Albany city directory of 1845, where he is identified as the "Architect of the Delavan House." He worked with civil engineer J. W. Adams on this project and is probably largely responsible for its Italianate design.

By 1851 William L. Woollett Jr. was successful enough to take on apprentices, including P. P. Saunders, who entered the office in that year and later worked as an architect and contractor in Poland, New York. In 1856 Woollett entered into partnership with Edward Ogden, who may have been a former apprentice as well. The firm was known as Woollett and Ogden until 1870 and was responsible for the design of several Albany churches.

William L. Woollett Jr. worked collaboratively with other architects throughout his career. Most prominent among these was Richard Upjohn, with whom Woollett undertook renovations to Lindenwald, Martin Van Buren's house in Kinderhook (1849). Woollett corresponded with Upjohn on issues pertaining to professional practice through the 1850s. In 1875 Richard's son Richard M. Upjohn and William's son William M. Woollett would work together on the construction of a Sunday school and chapel for St. Peter's Church in Albany.

Most of William L. Woollett Jr.'s Albany buildings have been lost. His best-known surviving works—Our Lady of Angels Roman Catholic Church, Emmanuel Baptist Church, and a delightful picturesque English Gothic chapel added to Frank Wills's Church of the Holy Innocents—all date from the period of his partnership with Edward Ogden.

Woollett designed suburban homes for several of Albany's prominent businessmen. These included Erastus Corning, for whom he designed a cottage, a farmer's cottage, and greenhouses in Bethlehem (1849), and John L. Schoolcraft, for whom he designed additions to his

Delavan House, Broadway between Steuben and Columbia streets. Albany Institute of History & Art Library.

home in Guilderland (1849–1850). With Edward Ogden Woollett produced designs for the Weare Coffin Little house in Menands (1868, demolished 1963) and with his son William M. designed renovations for the March-Stedman house in Loudonville (1870).

Additional commissions were located across New York State. In Trenton Falls he designed a hotel (1850–1851) and in Syracuse the New York State Asylum for Idiots (1854–1855), later the Syracuse State School. In Utica he designed the grand Italianate house Fountain Elms (1852, now part of the Munson-Williams-Proctor Arts Institute), two schools, an orphan asylum, and a Methodist church, and he entered a design competition for the city hall, won by Richard Upjohn.

A devout Methodist and resident of Loudonville, William L. Woollett Jr. served as superintendent of the Watervliet Union Sabbath School. He was also a trustee of the College of Missionaries at Syracuse University and president of the Albany YMCA. At the time of his death in 1874, Woollett's Albany Savings Bank, on the northwest corner of State and Chapel streets, was under construction. It was completed by his son William M. Woollett and Thomas Fuller, architect of the Capitol.

William M. Woollett was born in Albany. As a teenager he apprenticed with his father. He attended Rensselaer Polytechnic Institute and graduated with high honors from the Massachusetts Institute of Technology in 1870. He returned to Albany upon graduation and after his father's death carried on the practice in partnership with Franklin H. Janes. During his brief career William M. Woollett became a conspicuous local and even national figure. Like his father before him, William M. Woollett provided designs for houses and institutions associated with Albany's leading businessmen. With Janes he prepared designs for the Bacon-Stickney house in Loudonville (1874, demolished), the Jermain Memorial Church in Watervliet (1876), a cottage for C. D. Tillinghast in Menands (c. 1877, demolished), and the Home for Aged Men, a remodeling of the Menand house, in Menands (1877–1878).

William M. Woollett's trio of imposing Queen Anne brick villas on Englewood Place, overlooking Washington Park, all appeared in the pages of *American Architect and Building News*. A. J. Bicknell published some of Woollett's designs in *Wooden and Brick Buildings* in 1875 and then issued two volumes of Woollett's work, *Villas and Cottages or Homes for All* in 1876 and *Old Homes Made New* in 1878. William A. Wheeler, a draftsman in the office and later a partner in Fuller and Wheeler, executed many of the perspective views in *Old Homes Made New*. Woollett

William M. Woollett, designs for house fronts. A. J. Bicknell, Wooden and Brick Buildings *(New York: A. J. Bicknell and Company, 1875). New York State Library.*

was ill during the last three years of his life and died from tuberculosis in 1880 at 30. His Calvary Baptist Church on State Street near the Capitol was completed by Franklin Janes, who took over the practice in 1879.

William M. Woollett's children were still young when he died, but two grew up to become architects. William Lee Woollett (1872–1953) graduated from MIT, apprenticed with architects Fehmer and Page in Boston, and returned to Albany to set up his own practice. In 1905 his younger brother John Woollett joined his Albany office, and the firm designed several prominent buildings in Troy, including the Caldwell Apartments and the Rensselaer Hotel. In 1909 William moved to California, where in the wake of the San Francisco earthquake of 1906 there were many new opportunities for architects. John joined him soon afterward and eventually became California state architect. William Lee Woollett designed many distinctive Art Deco theaters in Hollywood and was involved in the construction of the Hollywood Bowl, as well as schools, offices, and residences. His son William Woollett and grandson Joseph L. Woollett have followed the extraordinary family tradition as architects, both in California.

Building List

William L. Woollett Jr.

1845   Delavan House (with J. W. Adams), Broadway bet. Steuben St. and Columbia St., burned 1894, demolished

1847   "Temple of Fancy" for Richard Pease, 516 Broadway

1849   Building for James Kidd, possibly 53–57 N. Pearl St.

1849   Engine house and hose depot, 739 Hamilton St., demolished

1849   Erastus Corning House, 102 State St., alterations, demolished

1850–1851   Delavan Stores, west side of Broadway bet. Hamilton St. and Pruyn St., demolished

1851   Albany Hospital, cor. of Lydius St. (now Madison Ave.) and Dove St., demolished

1851   Public school, Western Ave. at State St., demolished

1851–1852   N. Pearl St. Methodist Church, east side of N. Pearl St. bet. Columbia St. and Van Tromp St., demolished

1852   Orphan asylum, west side of Robin St. bet. Washington Ave. and Western Ave., additions and remodeling, demolished 1907

1852   Two townhouses for Blandina Dudley on Pearl St., probably demolished

1854–1857   Geological Hall, SW cor. of State St. and Lodge St., demolished c. 1937

1857   Design for a "temple" for a statue by Erastus Dow Palmer

William L. Woollett Jr. and Edward Ogden

1852–1856   Dudley Observatory, Dudley Park, after designs by A. J. Downing and Calvert Vaux, demolished

1858   Bridgford Vault, Albany Rural Cemetery

1858   School 12, east side of intersection of Washington Ave., Western Ave., and Robin St., demolished c. 1904

1860   Tweedle Building, cor. of State St. and Pearl St., burned 1883, partially rebuilt, demolished c. 1915

1863–1865   Ash Grove Methodist Church and parsonage, SW cor. of Ash Grove Pl. and Trinity Pl., demolished c. 1910

1865–1866   Hudson St. Methodist Episcopal Church, alterations, Hudson St. bet. Grand St. and Philip St., demolished

1866   Chapel (and schoolhouse?), Church of the Holy Innocents, SE cor. of N. Pearl St. and Colonie St.

1868–1869   First Congregational Church, SE cor. of Eagle St. and Beaver St., demolished

1869   New City Building, SW cor. of S. Pearl St. and Howard St., demolished

1869   Our Lady of Angels Roman Catholic Church, cor. of Central Ave. and Robin St.

1869–1871   Emmanuel Baptist Church, 275 State St.

William L. Woollett Jr. (with William M. Woollett)

1874–1875   Albany Savings Bank, NW cor. of State St. and Chapel St., completed by William M. Woollett with Thomas Fuller, demolished

William M. Woollett and Franklin H. Janes

1874   Corning carriage house, renovations, Howard St., demolished

1875–1876   Sunday school and chapel for St. Peter's Church, Chapel St., as supervising architect for Richard M. Upjohn, demolished

c. 1878   Benjamin W. Wooster House, 1 Englewood Pl.

c. 1879   Henry Russell House, 3 Englewood Pl.

c. 1879   Oscar L. Hascy House, 2 Englewood Pl., demolished

pre-1880   Fort Building, SE cor. of State St. and Broadway, demolished

1880–1882   Calvary Baptist Church, SE cor. of State St. and High St., burned after 1915, demolished

William Lee Woollett

1899   Row houses, 43–45 Ten Broeck St.

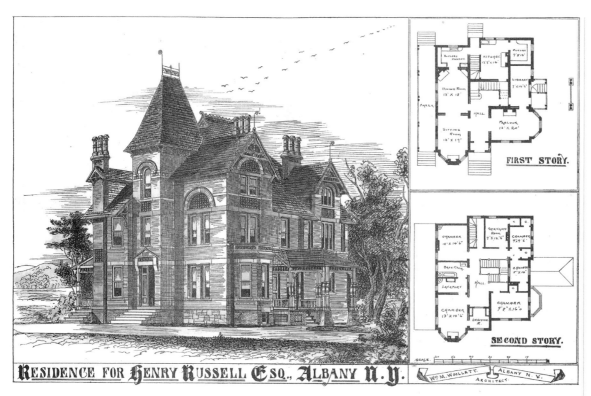

RESIDENCE FOR HENRY RUSSELL ESQ., ALBANY N.Y.

FIRST STORY.

SECOND STORY.

Wm M. WOOLLETT, ALBANY N.Y. ARCHITECT.

Henry Russell House, 3 Englewood Place.
American Architect and Building News,
October 18, 1879.

Albany Savings Bank, corner of State and Chapel streets. The Industries of the City of Albany (Albany: Elstner Publishing Company, 1889). Albany Public Library.

Benjamin W. Wooster House, 1 Englewood Place. Photograph provided by M. McCarty and G. Gold.

Patrick C. Keely

Cornelia Brooke Gilder

In the second half of the nineteenth century nearly every town and cityscape in the Northeast was dominated by a Roman Catholic church designed by Brooklyn-based ecclesiastical architect Patrick Keely (1816–1896). The son of an established Irish architect in Tipperary, the young Keely immigrated in 1842, just before the potato famine that would bring so many of his compatriots to the United States. Over his 50-year career he designed as many as 600 churches in North America, from Prince Edward Island to New Orleans and from Newport, Rhode Island, to Watertown, Wisconsin.

Saint Joseph's Roman Catholic Church, corner of First and Ten Broeck streets. Photograph provided by M. McCarty and G. Gold. Interior, New York Public Library.

Keely was only 32 years old in 1848 when the Diocese of Albany hired him to design his first cathedral. Known as the Cathedral of the Immaculate Conception, this imposing, twin-spired brownstone Gothic structure now stands as a dramatic foil to the sleek, marble-clad Empire State Plaza. A follower of the great Victorian architect Augustus W. Pugin, Keely specified for Albany's cathedral, as well as for later projects, stained glass from the Birmingham, England, studio of John Hardman and Company, where Pugin was the principal designer.

After his start in Albany, Keely went on to design 15 more cathedrals, beginning with Buffalo in 1851–1852. Others were built in Portland, Maine (1866–1869); Boston (1866–1875); Chicago (1874–1875); Springfield, Massachusetts (1875); Hartford, Connecticut (1875–1892, burned 1956); and Providence, Rhode Island (1893), as well as Fall River, Massachusetts. His grandest cathedral, in Brooklyn, was begun but never completed.

Designing for parishes with limited budgets and inexperienced building committees often hampered Keely's ambitious proposals. In Albany, however, St. Joseph's Church in Arbor Hill (1856–1860) is a magnificent example of his use of lavish materials and craftsmanship. The bluestone facades were originally trimmed in French Caen stone, which was soon replaced with more-enduring Indiana limestone. Inside, the hammer-beam roof, embellished with angels, is worthy of an architect whose first love was woodcarving. At his first Brooklyn church, Sts. Peter and Paul in Williamsburg (1847–1848), Keely carved the reredos himself.

With hundreds of churches to his name, Keely certainly reused successful designs. In 1865 he provided plans similar to St. Joseph's in Albany for Hartford's Asylum Hill Congregational Church, a rare Protestant project. He also tried fresh ideas, materials, and designs. The Church of the Immaculate Conception in Boston (1861) is Classical Revival; St. Joseph's Church on Tulane Avenue in New Orleans (1869) is one of his first

Romanesque designs; and St. Bernard's in Greenwich Village in New York City (1875) is Ruskinian Gothic.

A committed family man and father of 17, Keely brought three sons and two sons-in-law into his busy Brooklyn practice. In Catholic circles Keely was highly regarded during his long lifetime, with Notre Dame University awarding him the prestigious Laerte Medal in 1884. However, the mainstream press and later critics either ignored or belittled him. With thousands of New Yorkers worshipping in his grand, vaulted sanctuaries, Patrick C. Keely's passing in 1896 elicited scant mention in the *New York Times*.

Building List

1848–1852 Cathedral of the Immaculate Conception, SW cor. of Eagle St. and Madison Ave.
1856–1860 St. Joseph's Roman Catholic Church, NW cor. of First St. and Ten Broeck St.

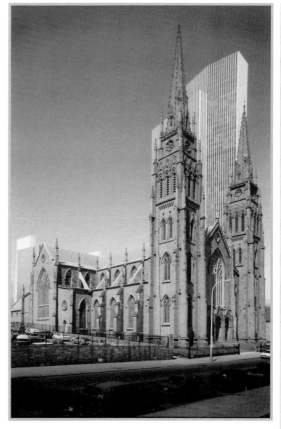

Cathedral of the Immaculate Conception, corner of Eagle Street and Madison Avenue. Photograph provided by M. McCarty and G. Gold.

Cathedral of the Immaculate Conception. Mesick Cohen Wilson Baker Architects.

Frank Wills

Cornelia Brooke Gilder

The design of lofty Gothic Anglican churches in the mid-nineteenth century made the careers of New York architects like Richard Upjohn and James Renwick Jr. Their contemporary, Frank Wills (1822–1856), died too young to be ranked with them. However, in his day Wills, as an architect and a writer, was an influential figure in the American Gothic Revival movement.

Like Upjohn, Wills was an Englishman. He was trained in Exeter and came to New York City via Canada under the patronage of a compatriot, Bishop John Medley of New Brunswick. Two imposing Canadian cathedrals stand as bookends to Wills's career. The first, Christ Church Anglican Cathedral in Fredericton, New Brunswick, was begun in 1845, when Wills was 23 years old. The second, Christ Cathedral of Montreal, was begun in 1856, the year of Wills' untimely death, and completed in 1860.

In between the Canadian commissions, Wills practiced in New York City, mostly on his own and briefly (1852–1853) with Henry C. Dudley, another English architect from Exeter. During his New York years Wills became an editor of *The New York Ecclesiologist* and wrote *Ancient English Ecclesiastical Architecture* (1850). Through these publications, he advocated the use of English medieval styles for the growing Episcopal movement in America, responding to the "unchurchlike" colonial forms of the Puritans.

Wills designed several substantial, spired stone churches, including the House of Prayer Episcopal Church (1850) in Newark, New Jersey, and St. Peter's Church (1853) in Milford, Connecticut. But he had greater success with less costly, smaller churches, like his two buildings in Albany, the Church of the Holy Innocents (1849) and Grace Church (1850). "If you cannot build a good tower, build none at all," recommended Wills in *Ancient English Ecclesiastical Architecture*. At the Church of the Holy Innocents, which still stands at 275 North Pearl Street in Arbor Hill, Wills carried the front gable up to a decorative bell cote. "Be not ashamed of rough stone walls if you have no money to spend on polished marble," Wills declared. At Holy Innocents he trimmed rough bluestone with finished sandstone. Now deserted, the church still retains its original stained glass by Wills's favored New York City glassmaker, John Jay Bolton. Architects Woolett and Ogden designed the picturesque attached chapel in 1866, employing Wills's same choice of materials and Gothic spirit.

Even with the most modest structure, Wills delighted in designing features with medieval precedents. Grace Church was a board-and-batten structure designed for the corner of Washington Avenue and Lark Street in Albany. In order to grant prominence to the bell turret, Wills placed it over the chancel archway in "the position of the ancient sancte bell." This church was moved to the corner of Clinton Avenue and Robin Street in 1873 and burned in 1951.

Wills's two Albany churches were published in *Ancient English Ecclesiastical Architecture*. A number of similar Episcopal churches by this important Anglican revivalist still grace communities from Oberlin, Ohio, to Annandale, Mississippi.

Building List

1849 Church of the Holy Innocents, cor. of N. Pearl St. and Colonie St.
1850 Grace Church, cor. of Washington Ave. and Lark St., moved, demolished

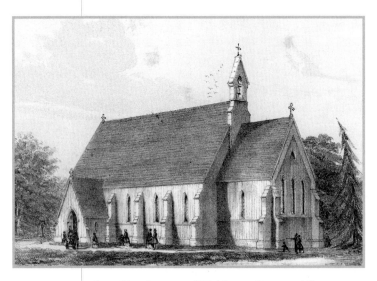

Grace Church, corner of Washington Avenue and State Street. Frank Wills, Ancient English Ecclesiastical Architecture and Its Principles *(New York: Stanford and Swords, 1850). New York State Library.*

Church of the Holy Innocents, corner of North Pearl and Colonie streets. Frank Wills,
Ancient English Ecclesiastical Architecture and Its Principles *(New York: Stanford and Swords, 1850). New York State Library.*

Church of the Holy Innocents. Albany Institute of History & Art Library.

Ogden & Ogden

Lewis C. Rubenstein

The Ogdens, father and son, spanned 70 years of the most fruitful era for Albany architecture. They designed numerous significant buildings and collaborated with one leading architectural figure after another.

The name of Edward Ogden, architect, first entered the Albany city directory in 1853. It remained there for almost half a century, linked from 1856 to 1870 with that of William L. Woollett Jr., from 1871 to 1889 with Frank P. Wright, and from 1891 to 1900 with Edward's son Charles.

The elder Ogden, Wright, and Woollett all were born in England. While Wright had six years of architectural training in England at an art school in Nottingham, Ogden, born in 1826, came to Albany as a boy at the age of 13. He apparently finished his apprenticeship in 1849 and worked for Woollett for several years before his name appeared on the letterhead.

Kenmore Hotel, 72–78 North Pearl Street.
The Industries of the City of Albany
(Albany: Elstner Publishing Company,
1889). Albany Public Library.

Well connected politically and socially and active in the Albany Cricket Club, the Albany Curling Club, the Van Rensselaer Guard, the St. George Society, the Caledonian Society, and the Burns Club, Ogden was in an excellent position to further his professional interests. He was superintendent of construction and one of the supervising architects of the U.S. Post Office and Federal Building (now part of the headquarters of the State University of New York) at the foot of State Street on Broadway, and his firms were given commissions for a number of other public buildings, as well as for industrial plants, carriage-trade stores, offices, and churches, both Catholic and Protestant. According to his obituary he designed "many of the most handsome private dwellings in our city."

The various Ogden firms seemed most at home with brick. As indicated by the Kenmore Hotel, the State Normal School, and other buildings with steeply pitched gables and strong emphasis on the vertical line, their buildings appear to have been seeking a style and material in keeping with the city's origins. Albanians of the 1880s and 1890s saw their architecture, particularly in the North Pearl Street shopping district, as being "correct but always advanced in its taste, combining with the rush and bustle of the modern business activity the quiet ways of good breeding and refinement."

Edward's son Charles was born in 1858 and educated at Albany private schools, graduating from the Albany Academy in 1874. The following year, at the age of 18, he entered his father's firm as an apprentice. Two years later he gained a listing in the Albany city directory as a draftsman.

Charles Ogden's marriage in 1884 to Lizzie Kinnear could only have helped his career. His father-in-law, Peter Kinnear, was an Albany industrialist active in politics. Commissions for public and industrial buildings, including a factory for Kinnear's Albany Billiard Ball Company, continued to come to Charles Ogden after his father died in 1900.

During the early years of the twentieth century Charles practiced without a partner. An association with Walter H. Van Guysling, who had assisted him as an apprentice on the Keeler's Restaurant project, appears to have been short lived. In 1916, however, Ogden, along with Joseph J. Gander, won the commission for redesigning the interiors of the Albany City Hall. This partnership with Joseph Gander and later with John P. and Conrad Gander lasted until 1926. At that time, aged 68, Charles Ogden retired because of poor health. In September 1931, as Gander, Gander, and Gander began work on designs for the new main post office, Charles wrote from his new home in Rye, New York, offering assistance. He died within a day or two of sending the letter.

Sometimes the fates seem to be against the Ogdens' major works in Albany: the New York State Normal School burned; the John G. Myers store collapsed while extensive renovations were underway; the J. B. Lyon Block came down for the Empire State Plaza. In the late twentieth century, however, the name Ogden was well known: Ogden's was for many years the name of one of Albany's fanciest restaurants. Fortunately for that restaurant, which was located in the former Home Telephone Company, as well as for the family's enduring fame, Edward, upon arrival in the U.S., changed his last name. In England the name had been Hogben.

Building List

Woollett and Ogden (1856–1870) See the Woolletts

Ogden and Wright (1871–1891)
 1871 School No. 15, Franklin St. and Herkimer St., demolished
 1873 School No. 11, 409 Madison Ave.
 1874–1876 Albany High School, Eagle St. bet. Steuben St. and Columbia St., demolished
 1876 Fifth Precinct Station, 220 Central Ave., demolished
 1878 Kenmore Hotel, 72–78 N. Pearl St., improvements and expansion, 1891
 1884 John G. Myers Block, 39–41 N. Pearl St., collapsed 1905, demolished
 1884–1885 New York State Normal School, Willett St., burned 1906, demolished
 c. 1886 Albany Paper Box Factory, 293 Broadway, demolished
 1886–1887 Marshall Tebbutt House, 483 State St.
 1887 Albany Business College, NE cor. of N. Pearl St. and Columbia St.
 1887 McPherson Terrace row houses, Clinton Ave., extended c. 1891
 1890 Bainbridge Burdick House, 935 Madison Ave.
 c. 1890 Eugene R. Hartt House, 407 State St.
 c. 1890 William B. Elmendorf House, 1001 Madison Ave.

Albany Home Telephone Company, corner of Howard and Lodge streets. Photograph provided by M. McCarty and G. Gold.

"Brides Row," 144–170 Chestnut Street. Photograph provided by M. McCarty and G. Gold.

Edward Ogden and Son (1891–1900)

1891   James McKinney House (now St. Andrew's Society), 150 Washington Ave.

1892   Dr. Frederick C. Curtis House, 17 Washington Ave., demolished

1892–1893   School No. 4, cor. of Madison Ave. and Ontario St., burned, demolished

1893   J. B. Lyon Block, Hudson Ave., Market Square, expansion 1907, demolished

c. 1894   Lewis E. Carr House, 923 Madison Ave.

1894?   YMCA, extension, cor. of Steuben St. and Chapel St.

pre-1895   Convent of Our Lady of Angels, 183 Central Ave.

pre-1895   Convent of Little Sisters of the Poor, 391 Central Ave., demolished 1977

1895   P. A. Elliott House, 34 N. Allen St.

c. 1896   Residence, 147 S. Lake Ave.

1896   Albany Waterworks, remodeling of office building, Quackenbush St.

1897   F. A. McNamee House, 690 Madison Ave.

1897   Madison Avenue Presbyterian Church, 820 Madison Ave.

1897   St. Andrew's Episcopal Church, cor. of Western Ave. and Main Ave., demolished 1956

pre-1898   Albany Railroad Co., Quail St., demolished

pre-1898   Arthur Mills House, 155 Lake Ave.

pre-1898   Drislane Store, 144–170 S. Pearl St.?, demolished

1899   Municipal Gas Co. Building, 112 State St., demolished

1899-1900   "Brides Row," 144–170 Chestnut St.

c. 1900   Wing Brothers and Hartt factory, Dallius St. bet. Rensselaer St. and Mulberry St., demolished

Charles Ogden (1900–1915)

1901   American Cigar Co. factory, cor. of Arch St. and Grand St.

pre-1903   C. O. Hasselbarth factory, Hamilton St. bet. Union St. and Liberty St., demolished

1903   Albany Home Telephone Co., SW cor. of Howard St. and Lodge St.

1903   Hospital for Incurables, new wings, McCarty Ave., demolished

1903   Residence, 102 S. Lake Ave.

1903–1908   St. John's Roman Catholic Church, cor. of Green St. and Westerlo St.

c. 1903   St. Andrew's Society Hall, Howard St. near Eagle St., demolished

c. 1904   Keeler's Restaurant (with Walter H. Van Guysling), alterations, 56 State St., demolished

1905   YWCA Building, alterations, cor. of Lodge St. and Steuben St., c. 1915, demolished

1907   Hudson River Day Line Ticket Office (with Walter H. Van Guysling), 351 Broadway

1908   Dr. Joseph Ivimey Dowling House (with Walter H. Van Guysling), 116 Washington Ave., demolished

1908   St. Anthony's Roman Catholic Church, SE cor. of Grand St. and Madison Ave.

c. 1908   Albany Billiard Ball Co., 483 Delaware Ave., demolished

1913   Fuld and Hatch Knitting Co., cor. of Liberty St. and Hamilton St.

1914   Academy of Holy Names (now part of Albany Medical Center), 628 Madison Ave.

Attributed to Charles Ogden

c. 1886   Charles Ogden House, 112 S. Lake Ave.

c. 1886   Residence, 114 S. Lake Ave.

Ogden and Gander (1916–1926) *See Gander, Gander & Gander*

Walter Dickson

Jessica Fisher Neidl

Although contemporary sources credit architect Walter Dickson (1834–1903) with executing "important commissions" in Albany during the second half of the nineteenth century, one is hard pressed to find more than the one extant building that can be attributed to him—the freestanding Romanesque residence that Dickson built for himself at 503 State Street in 1886.

The son of Scottish immigrants, Dickson was born in Albany on September 11, 1834. He attended the Albany Academy from 1846 to 1849, where he exhibited a talent for drawing. Following high school he served apprenticeships in the offices of Albany architects William Ellis and William L. Woollett before spending a year in New York City, where he continued his education under architect John B. Snook.

Upon his return to Albany in 1854, Dickson established an architectural practice, working out of his parents' house. Within a few years he had an office on State Street, working as both an architect and a real-estate broker. In 1864 he designed and oversaw the construction of the temporary Army Relief Bazaar building in Academy Park, and in 1866 he entered the competition for the design of the New York State Capitol, losing the commission to Thomas Fuller.

A year later Dickson took a decade-long hiatus from architecture and went to work for his brother-in-law at Taylor and Son's Brewery. Dickson resumed his architectural practice in 1877, and from 1878 to 1885 he superintended the construction of the U.S. Post Office and Federal Building on Broadway at the foot of State Street, seeing the project through to completion.

Years of hard work and his position at the Federal Building allowed Dickson to build the house at 503 State Street. The fortress-like building, faced with diaper brickwork, commands a flatiron-shaped lot overlooking the northwest corner of Washington Park and stands in horizontal contrast to the vertical townhouses that define the rest of the block. Dickson also designed three brick townhouses at 196, 198, and 200 Washington Avenue (c. 1884), which were united and converted in the early 1890s to serve as a bank, the purpose it continues to serve today. The unifying facade of the building is a late work of Albert Fuller and was erected in the early 1920s, but Dickson's original west sidewall, the rear wall, and the roofline of 200 Washington are still visible. Another residence, a brick, shingle, and half-timbered house located at 116 South Lake Avenue that dates to 1886, is also attributed to Dickson.

That same year Dickson served as head of the historical committee for Albany's bicentennial celebration. Under this commission he researched and designed 42 bronze memorial tablets placed at various locations throughout downtown, commemorating places and events of historical interest, particularly from the city's earliest days. More than a dozen of these tablets remain today, including those at City Hall; St. Mary's Roman Catholic Church at Pine and Lodge streets; the Mechanics' and Farmers' Bank at State and James streets; "Lydius Corner," the northeast corner of State and North Pearl streets; and the site of the old Fort Frederick, at the head of State Street below the Capitol. Many of the plaques have disappeared or have been moved

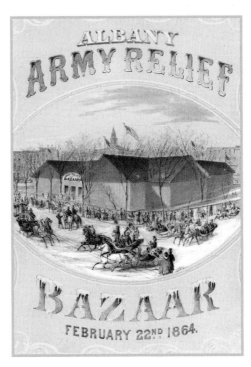

Army Relief Bazaar, Academy Park. Courtesy of Norman S. Rice.

196, 198, and 200 Washington Avenue. American Architect and Building News, *January 17, 1885.*

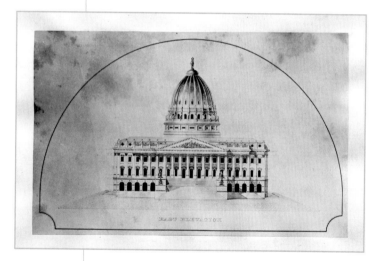

Walter Dickson, competition drawing for New York State Capitol. New York State Library.

503 State Street, entrance. Photograph provided by M. McCarty and G. Gold.

over the years as buildings were razed and the streetscape altered.

In 1887 Dickson formed a partnership with New York City architect Frederick Clarke Withers, and two years later Dickson sold his house on State Street and moved his family to Brooklyn. For the remainder of his career he worked largely on institutional buildings in and around New York City, though work did bring him back to Albany in 1891, when the firm of Withers and Dickson was engaged to undertake alterations to the Cathedral of the Immaculate Conception.

Though this native son apparently left little physical mark on his hometown, Dickson was, nevertheless, a prominent figure in Albany society. He was a member and one-time president of the St. Andrew's Society, an officer in the Albany Society of New York, and a member of the Fort Orange Club and the Albany Burgesses Corps. He was also the first president of the Electric Illuminating Company in Albany. He was, by all accounts, a very charismatic man.

Though only a very few buildings in Albany known to be associated with Walter Dickson exist today, he was described upon his death on September 3, 1903, by the *American Architect and Building News* as "one of the best-known architects in New York State." He is buried in Green-Wood Cemetery in Brooklyn.

Building List

1864 Army Relief Bazaar, Academy Park, demolished
1878–1885 U.S. Post Office and Federal Building, Broadway (superintendent of construction)
c. 1884 196, 198, and 200 Washington Ave.
1886 503 State St.
1886 116 S. Lake Ave. (attributed)
1886 Albany Bicentennial Celebration memorial tablets

Richard Upjohn and Richard M. Upjohn

Cornelia Brooke Gilder

Albany's extraordinary bluestone St. Peter's Episcopal Church, *gracing a prominent State Street corner, brings together the overlapping careers of the Upjohn father and son in a single, striking landmark.*

When hired by the Albany congregation in 1859, the portly, middle-aged Richard Upjohn (1802–1878) was probably America's most influential ecclesiastical architect. He had immigrated here in his late twenties from Dorset, England, where he began as an apprentice to a cabinetmaker and builder. He and his wife and baby son, Richard Mitchell, first settled in New Bedford, Massachusetts, and in 1833 moved to Boston, where he worked with architect Alexander Parris. Upjohn's first Gothic church was the wood frame St. John's Episcopal in Bangor, Maine (1837–1839), and soon afterward he made his name in New York City with the construction of Wall Street's lofty brownstone Trinity Church (1839–1846).

In the 1840s and 1850s, in between the completion of Trinity Church and the construction of St. Peter's in Albany, Upjohn not only designed well-appointed big-city churches but also provided scores of poor rural congregations with plans for easily built, picturesque, board-and-batten Gothic places of worship. His pattern book entitled *Rural Architecture* (1852) included plans for churches, chapels, rectories, and schools. A devout Episcopalian, Upjohn was a follower of the British Ecclesiological Society, which sought to link architecture and spirituality. In his ecclesiastical work Upjohn designed almost exclusively Episcopalian churches, even refusing on one occasion to accept a commission for a Unitarian church in Boston. He had a predilection toward the Gothic Revival but also designed notable buildings in other styles, like the Romanesque Bowdoin College Chapel and Library (1845–1855) and the Italianate St. Paul's Church in Baltimore (1855–1856).

Aside from his many churches, Upjohn was sought after as a residential architect. In the Upper Hudson Valley he made alterations to two distinguished houses—the Van Rensselaer Manor House north of Albany (1840–1843) and Martin Van Buren's Lindenwald in Kinderhook (1849–1850). A founder of the American Institute of Architects, Upjohn served as the organization's first president, from 1857 to 1876.

Upjohn's son, Richard M. (1828–1903), began working as a draftsman for his father and at the age of 22 managed the office for a year when the senior Upjohn went abroad. On his return in 1851 Upjohn made his son a partner. By the late 1850s, when St. Peter's was designed, the younger Upjohn was increasingly involved in the firm's

Saint Peter's Episcopal Church, corner of State and Lodge streets. Photograph provided by M. McCarty and G. Gold.

Saint Peter's Episcopal Church. New York State Library.

major commissions, some of which were in more distant places, including three in Alabama. The younger Upjohn is credited with St. Mark's in San Antonio, Texas, begun the same year as St. Peter's in Albany.

St. Peter's may have been a father-son collaboration, but the distinctive High Victorian tower (1876), made possible by a later bequest, was definitely the work of the son. Having received more formal education than his father, Richard M. Upjohn's ability to draw is considered superior to that of his famous father, and his surviving drawing for the tower of St. Peter's demonstrates his skill.

Although his career was always in the shadow of his father, Richard M. Upjohn was the architect of one formidable New England landmark, the Connecticut State Capitol in Hartford (1872–1878), a highly decorated Victorian Gothic structure with a tall, ornamented dome.

The Upjohn architectural dynasty continued into the third generation with the career of Richard M. Upjohn's son, Hobart.

Building List

1859–1861   St. Peter's Episcopal Church, NW cor. of State St. and Lodge St., tower added 1876

Nichols & Brown

Willow Partington

The prolific partnership of two mid-nineteenth-century church architects, Charles C. Nichols (1840–1898) and Frederick W. Brown, appears from city directories to have been confined to a six-year period, from 1864 to 1870. During this time they executed at least five churches in Albany, as well as several in New England, including the Fourth Presbyterian Church (1866–1868) in Middletown, Connecticut, and the Second Congregational Church (1868–1870) in New London, Connecticut.

Little biographical information is known about either Nichols or Brown. The senior partner, Nichols, was born in Alford, Massachusetts, and according to city directories began his career in Albany as a builder. During Nichols and Brown's partnership Thomas Fuller joined them briefly when he first arrived in Albany from Ottawa to work on the state Capitol. For one year, 1869, both firms—Fuller, Nichols and Company, and Nichols and Brown—were listed at 67 State Street.

Today Nichols and Brown's only known surviving Albany churches are the Gothic St. Ann's Roman Catholic Church (1867–1868) in the South End and the Romanesque Revival St. Mary's (1869), located behind the New York State Court Appeals. After 1870 the two architects worked independently, teaming up occasionally as in 1879–1880 and again in 1882, but little is known about their later work. From 1873 to 1878 Nichols was in partnership with John B. Halcott, one of his former draftsmen. Brown had partners only occasionally, namely Clarence Cutler in 1877 and Walter Dawson in 1886. According to a 1963 article by Kermit C. Parsons in the *Journal of the Society of Architectural Historians*, some buildings at Cornell University were also designed by Nichols and Brown. At least one of these was built, Llenroc, the 1867 villa of Ezra Cornell.

In writing about the construction of a new rectory for Trinity Church, located on Broad Street (now Trinity Place) below Madison Avenue, Joel Munsell noted that "Messrs. Nichols & Brown of this city were engaged as architects to prepare the plans and specifications for the proposed building, which was generously done on their part, *without charge*." This largess came around 1867 as the contract for excavating the site, stone cutting, iron lintels, and other such work was given in that year. One William Nichols was given the contract for the "putting on of the timber, and other carpenter work," but his relationship to Charles C. Nichols is unknown.

Outside Albany, Nichols designed St. Joseph's French

Church in Cohoes in 1874. In 1886 one of his few known domestic commissions, a row of handsome Queen Anne houses on State Street, was published in *L'Architecture Americaine*. Frederick Brown appears to have left Albany in the early 1890s, but Nichols continued to practice here until his death, on March 27, 1898. His brief obituary in the *Times Union* described him extravagantly as one of the best-known architects in the U.S.

Saint Mary's Roman Catholic Church, Lodge Street. Photograph provided by M. McCarty and G. Gold.

Malcomb Row, State Street. Photograph by Joe Putrock.

Building List

Nichols and Brown

1862   State Street Presbyterian Church (later Westminster Presbyterian Church), State St., burned, interior rebuilt

1865–1866   Fourth Presbyterian Church, Broadway bet. Clinton Ave. and Wilson St., demolished

c. 1867   Rectory for Trinity Episcopal Church, Trinity Pl. below Madison Ave.

1867–1868   St. Ann's Roman Catholic Church, cor. of Fourth Ave. and Franklin St.

1868   Methodist Episcopal Church, temporary wooden structure, cor. of Ten Broeck St. and Livingston Ave., demolished 1880

1869   St. Mary's Roman Catholic Church, Lodge St. (tower added 1893–1897, not to Nichols and Brown plans)

Charles C. Nichols

pre-1886   1–7 Malcomb Row, partially extant (now 249–255 State St.)

Attributed to Frederick Brown

1877–1878   Park View Terrace, 566–578 Madison Ave.

Capitol Architects

Thomas Fuller, Leopold Eidlitz, and Isaac Perry

Andrea J. Lazarski

Prominently situated on State Street hill, the imposing, gray granite New York State Capitol is executed in an eclectic French Renaissance Revival mode. The Capitol was created as the result of two design competitions, a series of architects, and political, financial, and architectural compromises made over the three decades of its construction.

Thomas Fuller (1823–1898) served as the first architect of the Capitol, from 1868 to 1876. Fuller resided in Canada and had established a career marked by notable commissions such as one of the Parliament buildings in Ottawa. He was among the few architects who entered the initial design competition for the New York State Capitol in 1863. The limited response may have been due to poor circulation of the advertisement and the lack of "compensation for preparing plans." Furthermore, at the time of the competition land for the building and construction funding had not yet been secured.

The outcome of the second design competition, held in 1866, created an uneasy partnership that merged Thomas Fuller's plans with elements of architect Arthur D. Gilman's proposal. This design was approved by Gov. Reuben Fenton in December 1867, but Gilman, nationally recognized for his Second Empire designs, withdrew after differences of opinion with Fuller. In April 1869 Fuller responded to suggestions from the Commissioners of the Capitol with a new design that reflected the influence of Augustus Laver, another architect who had entered the design competitions. Fuller's revised design was widely circulated in national publications in 1869 and 1870 and described as being in "the style of the pavilions of the New Louvre" with a "terrace which forms the grand approach to the east or principal front." The main entrance at the second-story level was reached by a flight of steps on the east, leading to suites for the governor, adjutant general, secretary of state, and attorney general. On the third floor were the chambers for the Senate and Assembly and the State Library. These rooms were planned as two-story spaces with ceiling heights of 48 feet. The remaining rooms on the third and fourth floors were reserved for committees and working offices. A 300-square-foot tower crowned the roofline. In the center of the building an open court, 137 feet by 92 feet in plan, provided light and air to the rooms within.

In May 1865 three "New Capitol Commissioners" were appointed by the Legislature to obtain plans for the building and supervise construction. These commissioners—citizens with little or no experience with architecture—were charged with construction oversight, the purchase of materials, and paying the workers. A decade later, in 1875, charges of mismanagement, wasted expenses, and unnecessary work stoppages were being investigated by several legislative committees. Fuller was asked to provide detailed plans and specifications of the legislative chambers and working drawings to complete the building before additional funding would be released.

As public denouncement of the "inartistic and extravagant architecture" increased, three nationally prominent design professionals—Leopold Eidlitz, Henry Hobson Richardson, and Frederick Law Olmsted—

Thomas Fuller, design for New York State Capitol. Harper's Weekly, *October 9, 1869.*

Leopold Eidlitz, design for New York State Capitol. American Architect and Building News, *April 15, 1876.*

New York State Capitol, east front, head of State Street. Photograph provided by M. McCarty and G. Gold.

were appointed to a new advisory board of architects to evaluate Fuller's design and construction management and to analyze the allocation and arrangement of space for offices, legislative chambers, and corridors. The advisory board criticized all aspects of Fuller's proposal, from the exterior design, interior staircases, and ceremonial spaces to the interior finishes. The report closed with the advisory board's presenting its own design solutions for the Capitol. Its recommendation to change the building from a Renaissance style to the Romanesque created a storm of controversy within the architectural community in New York and across the nation. Fuller was effective at garnering support from members of the American Institute of Architects but was unable to influence and survive the political forces in Albany.

In September 1876 a new firm—known as Eidlitz, Richardson, and Olmsted—was retained as the architects of the Capitol, replacing Fuller. Leopold Eidlitz (1823–1908), who was born in Prague and was trained as a land steward, emigrated to New York City in 1843. Eidlitz apprenticed in Richard Upjohn's office and within ten years had established his own practice, specializing in ecclesiastical work. As a founding member of the American Institute of Architects in 1857, Eidlitz engaged in debate on style, ethics, architectural training, and technology. His writings on aesthetics and architecture were frequently published in architectural journals and culminated in *The Nature and Function of Art, More Especially of Architecture*, published in 1881.

Eidlitz played a major role in proposing exterior changes to reflect the interior use of the rooms. The corner pavilions suggested major suites for the governor, secretary of state, and other dignitaries, while the north and south central rooflines marked the legislative chambers.

On the interior Eidlitz's work was concentrated in the north half of the building and the northeast and southeast staircases. The Assembly Chamber was the first ceremonial space to be completed (1879). Lavished with praise by architectural critics and the press, the soaring, sandstone-vaulted ceiling, which was decorated with gold, vermilion, and ultramarine, was proclaimed to be "the most monumental interior in the country." The Assembly Staircase (1878) echoed the color palette of the Assembly Chamber in the ornate stenciled walls terminating in a stained-glass laylight. On the second floor the Golden Corridor's gilded surfaces, enriched with reds and blues, were pronounced to be "pure splendor with no architectural decoration comparable." North of the Golden Corridor and one floor beneath the Assembly Chamber Eidlitz planned space for the Court of Appeals (1880).

Eidlitz's masterpiece, the Assembly Chamber, evidenced cracks in the vaulted ceiling within a year of its completion. Throughout the 1880s, as Eidlitz defended his design, the sandstone was replaced; the ceiling was repeatedly studied by experts; and the foundations were analyzed. In 1888 the ceiling was declared unsafe and replaced with a flat, coffered-wood ceiling. Few new commissions were awarded to Eidlitz thereafter.

Fourteen years after the start of construction, questions of cost, quality, and project duration were once again raised. The Capitol was still unfinished: two stories of the west pavilions, the east and west center sections, the northeast pavilion roofs, the tower, the portico, and the entrance terraces were not yet built. On the interior, staircases, courtrooms, and many offices awaited completion. In 1883, to remedy the slow pace, Gov. Grover Cleveland appointed Isaac Perry (1822–1908) as commissioner of the new Capitol. Perry, an architect-builder from Binghamton, had gained prominence in western New York after winning a design competition for the State Inebriate Asylum in Binghamton. Perry's design influence extended across New York State with the construction of over 40 armories in major regional centers and large-scale mental asylums. In Albany Perry remodeled the Executive Mansion on Eagle Street (1886–1887) into a picturesque Queen Anne-inspired residence. His design for the Washington Avenue Armory (1886–1892) became a prototype for smaller-scale armories.

Perry's first assignments at the Capitol were to implement the designs of Eidlitz and Richardson. The Senate Staircase (1885) had been designed by Eidlitz in a Romanesque mode with English Gothic details. Low-relief carving of wild creatures enhanced the sandstone pilasters and voussoirs rising to the skylight. Perry did not alter the original design, except for adding several round-arch openings in the staircase to increase natural light. He followed his predecessor's designs very closely, making only subtle changes, such as material substitutions, in Richardson's Court of Appeals (1884) and the State Library (1889).

Beginning with the Great Western Staircase (1896), Perry elaborated on his predecessor's designs: the plan of the staircase, for example, is clearly Richardson, but the extensive carving is the inspiration of Perry and his craftsman. Perry's eastern approach to the Capitol best demonstrates his own design capabilities and originality. The monumental staircase is flanked by terraces that connect the north and south porticoes. Granite carvings provide focal points throughout the stair to highlight historic and symbolic portraits and New York wildlife.

Perry had desired to balance the eastern approach with a lighter, copper-clad metal tower that would rise 50 feet above the roofline and 300 feet above street level. Perry's conception of the tower, like that of his predecessors, was quashed by a citizen commission with oversight on the Capitol construction. In 1899 at the age of 77, Isaac Perry was retired by Gov. Theodore Roosevelt.

New York State Capitol, Assembly Chamber. Courtesy of the New York State Commission on the Restoration of the Capitol.

New York State Capitol, Great Western Staircase. Courtesy of the New York State Commission on the Restoration of the Capitol.

Note: See also Henry Hobson Richardson, pages 28-29.

Henry Hobson Richardson

John I Mesick

In 1885 the nation's leading architectural magazine, American Architect and Building News, *conducted a survey of its readers to determine the ten most beautiful buildings in America. Five of the buildings selected were by one architect, Henry Hobson Richardson (1838-1886), and, of these, two were in Albany—the Capitol and the Albany City Hall.*

Richardson's architectural involvement with Albany commenced in 1875, when he assumed joint responsibility with Leopold Eidlitz for the completion of the Capitol. This work continued throughout the final decade of his brief career.

Albany City Hall, corner of Eagle and Pine streets. Photograph provided by M. McCarty and G. Gold.

The Capitol, first designed by Thomas Fuller in 1867, had become the subject of economic, political, and aesthetic controversies before it was half completed. In revising Fuller's scheme Richardson and Eidlitz attempted to resolve a difficult design on the exterior above the second story. While largely restricted to Fuller's floor plan and internal organization, the new architects had a freer hand in the architectural development of interior spaces. Richardson created some of his finest rooms here: the Senate Chamber (1881), the Court of Appeals (1881), and the Red Room in the governor's suite (1880) provided Richardson with the opportunity to produce the most opulent designs of his career. Richardson's designs for the Great Western Staircase (1884–1898) and the State Library (destroyed in the Capitol fire of 1911) were both completed by Isaac Perry following Richardson's death.

The city hall commission came to Richardson while he was working on the Capitol. In 1880 fire destroyed Philip Hooker's city hall of 1829. A tight budget prevented the full realization of Richardson's desires for this project. Later Richardson commented that when money was short, he preferred to spend it on the exterior and skimp on the interior. The Albany City Hall (1883) was a case in point; his modest interiors were reconstructed by Albany architects Ogden and Gander in 1916.

About the time city hall was nearing completion, Richardson undertook his third and final Albany building, a town house for Grange Sard Jr. (1885). It still stands at 397 State Street as part of an apartment complex.

Albany also presented Richardson with one of his greatest professional disappointments. His Romanesque competition design for the Cathedral of All Saints lost to the English Gothic project of Robert W. Gibson, which Episcopal Bishop William Croswell Doane favored. Richardson's All Saints design was an extraordinarily powerful composition in which the problems of adapting Romanesque ecclesiastical forms to the needs of a contemporary American cathedral were convincingly resolved. If this forceful cathedral had been erected on Capitol Hill instead of Gibson's more prosaic building, perhaps State Education Commissioner Andrew Draper would not have had the temerity two decades later to wrap the new Education Building around the cathedral site, thereby obscuring one of Albany's chief landmarks.

Richardson's mark on Albany was not confined to his four projects. In the two decades following 1880 numerous buildings in the "Richardsonian" style—massive stone structures with hipped roofs, triumphal entrance arches, and repetitive design elements—arose in Albany and the surrounding areas. Some notable examples are Fuller and Wheeler's Young Men's Christian Association on North Pearl Street, the Charles Ellis house in Schenectady, the Chapel and Crematory at Oakwood Cemetery in Troy, Isaac Perry's Washington Avenue Armory in Albany, and Temple Beth Emeth (now Wilborn Temple) on South Swan Street.

Hundreds of cities in the nation possess buildings bearing the mark of Richardson's influence. Albany was especially fertile ground because of the large number of stone carvers and masons who had come to Albany to work on the Capitol and surely were available from time to time to work on other buildings. Many Albany row houses—such as 26 and 28 Willett Street, 182 Washington Avenue, 304 State Street, and Ernest Hoffman's 333 State Street—exhibit rich Romanesque detail undoubtedly chiseled by stone carvers trained at the Capitol.

Court of Appeals Courtroom, now in New York State Court of Appeals, corner of Eagle and Pine streets. Photograph provided by M. McCarty and G. Gold.

Grange Sard House, 397 State Street. Photograph provided by M. McCarty and G. Gold.

Building List

1876–1883 New York State Capitol (with Leopold Eidlitz), head of State St. hill
1880–1883 Albany City Hall, cor. of Eagle St. and Pine St.
1881–1882 Robert H. Pruyn Memorial, Albany Rural Cemetery
1882–1885 Grange Sard House, 397 State St.

New York State Capitol, Senate Chamber, head of State Street hill. Courtesy of the New York State Commission on the Restoration of the Capitol.

Russell Sturgis

Cornelia Brooke Gilder

The erudite Russell Sturgis (1836–1909)—High Victorian Gothic architect, art critic, and compiler of an encyclopedic architectural dictionary—left his mark in Albany with a pair of polychrome townhouses (1873) in the fashionable residential area of upper State Street and a gem of a medieval bank building (1874–1875) on lower State Street in the city's commercial center.

Trained as an architect in Munich and inspired by the pre-Raphaelite ideas of John Ruskin, Sturgis established a practice in New York City, initially with Peter B. Wight in 1862. His name became synonymous with the creative and rich design and use of materials.

Learned and Norton houses, 298 and 300 State Street. Photograph provided by M. McCarty and G. Gold.

Sturgis's pair of Albany townhouses on the corner of State and Dove streets was built for two sisters, Katharine and Mary De Witt, and their husbands, Judge William L. Learned and John T. Norton. An angled corner tower on the Learned house and the gabled entries and arched windows trimmed with alternating bands of brick and stone distinguish this grouping. The same year that he was at work on these Albany houses, Sturgis also designed a pair of New York City townhouses at 4 and 6 West Fifty-seventh Street for brothers James A. Roosevelt and Theodore Roosevelt Sr. The Roosevelt houses were demolished long ago as Fifty-seventh Street became a commercial thoroughfare, but in Albany the Learned and Norton houses can still be seen in a residential context.

Built for the Mechanics' and Farmers' Bank, the delightful pressed-brick-and-sandstone structure at 63 State Street is a sliver of architectural sophistication. The ogee-arched front door and corbelled corner turret are worthy of a small Bavarian castle, and the ornate rose window in the side gable might have graced an ancient Old World church. The riot of carved ornamentation, quoins, and the elaborate cornice are all indicative of a prosperous client working with an imaginative designer. By the time Sturgis was working on the bank building in Albany, he had completed two brick-and-bluestone Gothic buildings at Yale (Farnam and Durfee residence halls) and was further defining the Old Campus quadrangle with the soaring Battell Chapel.

"Uninterrupted thought is not for the busy architect," wrote Sturgis in his later years. Juggling late-nineteenth-century pressures of plumbing and permits within short time schedules was not suited to the scholarly Sturgis. In the course of the 1880s he increasingly taught, wrote, and presided over organizations in Manhattan like the Architectural League and the Fine Arts Federation. He left active practice to the younger generation, including two sons, an architect, Danford, and a surveyor, Edward, and to many ascendant architects who had trained under him, including Charles McKim and William R. Mead.

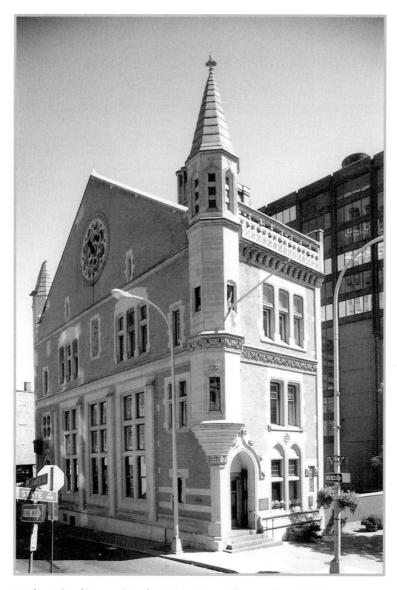

Mechanics' and Farmers' Bank, 63 State Street. Photograph provided by M. McCarty and G. Gold.

Sturgis's crowning accomplishment was *The Dictionary of Architecture and Building* (1901–1902). His own sons and many colleagues, including Robert W. Gibson, George L. Heins, Charles Platt, Montgomery Schuyler, and Ralph Adams Cram, contributed to this three-volume work, which is still in use today. His vast collection of architectural photographs is now owned by Washington University in St. Louis.

Building List

c. 1873 Learned and Norton houses, 298 and 300 State St.

1874–1875 Mechanics' and Farmers' Bank (now Center for Economic Growth), 63 State St.

Potter & Robertson

Cornelia Brooke Gilder

During the six-year period that these two High Victorian architects collaborated, Potter and Robertson designed three Queen Anne-style buildings in Albany, all for members of the influential Pruyn family.

The senior of the two architects, William Appleton Potter (1842–1909), was born in nearby Schenectady but grew up in Philadelphia, where his father, Alonzo, was the Episcopal bishop of Pennsylvania. Graduated from Union College in 1864, William Potter apprenticed in the New York architectural office of his half-brother, Edward Tuckerman Potter, before opening his own office in the early 1870s. His sister, Maria Louisa, married a talented Albany sculptor, Launt Thompson.

Charles L. Pruyn House, 44 Willett Street. American Architect and Building News, *July 3, 1880.*

Potter was well along in his career in 1875 when Robert H. Robertson (1849–1919) joined him. Potter's conspicuous and acclaimed library building at Princeton University (1871–1873) would lead to a decade of work on that campus, with five more commissions. Appointed supervising architect of the U.S. Treasury in 1875, Potter began to design a series of far-flung courthouses and post offices in Atlanta; Nashville; Fall River, Massachusetts; and Evansville, Indiana. He also designed an elaborate stone Federal Building for Albany in 1875. Its construction was stalled during Potter's tenure, and his successor, James Hill, reworked the exterior in the Renaissance Revival style. It stands at the foot of State Street on Broadway.

Born in Philadelphia and educated in Scotland and at Rutgers, Robert H. Robertson had also apprenticed with Edward T. Potter before joining William's firm. Working together from 1875 to 1881, Potter and Robertson produced ornate polychrome collegiate and commercial buildings, as well as private houses.

Their first completed project in Albany was a Queen Anne-style townhouse overlooking Washington Park at 38 Willett Street, built for businessman Robert Clarence Pruyn, a Rutgers contemporary of Robertson. Three years later his brother, Charles Lansing Pruyn, commissioned a second, more understated and classical house two doors south, at 44 Willett Street. Both houses were published in the *American Architect and Building News*, in 1877 and 1880. In the meantime their elderly father, Robert H. Pruyn, a noted lawyer, politician, diplomat, and banker, selected Potter and Robertson to redesign the facade of a commercial building at 70 North Pearl Street. An original, elegantly curved storefront still bears the architects' names and the construction date of 1879–1880. This facade of contrasting materials, ornamented gables, paneled chimney stacks, and terra-cotta decoration is typical of Potter and Robertson's richly textured buildings.

The two architects began practicing separately in the 1880s. Robertson was back in the Albany area in 1881 supervising the construction of a new brick Romanesque Revival office building for the Burden Iron Works in South Troy and remodeling the Burden family residence. Robertson went on to design townhouses for the Burdens in New York City. He also continued his relationship with the Pruyn family. In 1892–1893 he designed for Robert and Anna Pruyn a rustic retreat deep in the Adirondacks, which they called Santanoni.

Both Potter and Robertson were known for their picturesque churches. Potter designed many more Romanesque and Gothic structures at Princeton and buildings for Union College, Union Theological Seminary, and Columbia's Teachers College. At the turn of the century, Potter, still a bachelor, retired to Italy, long the home of his sister and brother-in-law, Launt Thompson. Potter was a leading figure in the American colony in Rome when he died there in 1909.

Robert H. Robertson practiced for another decade, into New York City's early skyscraper era. He also designed many country houses on Long Island (he and his family summered in Southampton), in Newport and in Lenox, and most notably in Shelburne, Vermont, where he designed the William and Lila Vanderbilt Webb house and its extraordinary farm complex. Late in life Robertson worked with R. B. Potter, his old partner's nephew, and his own architect son, T. Markoe Robertson.

Pruyn Building, 70 North Pearl Street. Photograph provided by M. McCarty and G. Gold.

U.S. Post Office and Federal Building, Broadway at foot of State Street. Photograph provided by M. McCarty and G. Gold.

Building List

William A. Potter

1875–1876 Design for U.S. Post Office and Federal Building, Broadway at foot of State St.

Potter and Robertson

1877 Robert C. Pruyn House, 38 Willett St.

1880 Charles L. Pruyn House, 44 Willett St.

1879–1880 Pruyn Building, 70 N. Pearl St.

Albert W. Fuller

T. Robins Brown

When Albert Fuller died in 1934, his obituary in the Times Union *called him the "dean of Albany architects." This designation reflected more than 50 years of active practice in Albany, during which time his firms were responsible for some of the city's most prominent structures.*

Born in 1854 in Clinton, New York, Fuller came to Albany as a youth and received his only known architectural training as a draftsman in the office of Ogden and Wright from 1873 to 1879. After a few years in St. Louis, where he designed three houses, Fuller returned to Albany and established the firm of Fuller and Wheeler in 1883 with William Arthur Wheeler, an Albanian who had studied with Boston architectural

YMCA Building, 60 North Pearl Street. The Industries of the City of Albany *(Albany: Elstner Publishing Company, 1889). Albany Public Library.*

firms. Fuller practiced alone from 1897 to 1900, then went into partnership from 1900 to 1904 with William B. Pitcher, a former draftsman in his office, and from 1910 to 1923 worked with William P. Robinson.

While Fuller's practice was most active in Albany and the vicinity, his firms also designed buildings in St. Louis, Denver, Scranton, Richmond, Washington, D.C., and Brockville, Ontario. Following the design of the Albany Young Men's Christian Association Building on North Pearl Street (1886–1887), Fuller and Wheeler designed YMCAs in Hartford, Connecticut; Montreal; and Oakland, California, and assisted in the design of the YMCA in Paris, France. The firm also designed numerous educational buildings, including six schools in Albany; the Auburn, New York, high school; and state normal schools in Plattsburgh and Oneonta. Fuller's last commission was the Bethlehem Central High School, erected in Delmar in 1932.

Eleven times between 1881 and 1918 buildings designed by Fuller's firms were published in national architectural magazines. In addition, Fuller's book, *Artistic Homes*, a compilation of his designs, was revised and issued five times between 1882 and 1891.

Fuller's buildings were competently designed, excellently constructed (in part due to his careful site supervision), and comfortably up-to-date in the accepted styles of the day. He typifies the eclectic late-nineteenth-century architect who readily adapted to changing architectural tastes. His firm's public buildings of the 1880s reflect the influence of Richardsonian Romanesque architecture, while domestic designs employed the Queen Anne, Shingle Style, and Colonial Revival idioms. The plan of the handsome Shingle Style house in Northeast Harbor, Maine, that Fuller and Wheeler designed for Erastus Corning Jr. was most surely influenced by the plan of Richardson's house for Dr. John Bryant of 1880. As architectural tastes changed in the 1890s to favor symmetry and formality, Fuller employed Renaissance Revival styles and, later, the Colonial Revival, as seen in the Harmanus Bleecker Library, erected in 1923–1924.

Fuller was a founder of the Albany Club, a member of the Fort Orange Club and the Albany Country Club, and a member and trustee of the First Presbyterian Church. In the 1880s he lived at 271 Lark Street and in the 1890s at 497 State Street, a house he probably designed for himself. His country residence in Castleton was still owned by his descendants in 1978.

Building List

Albert Fuller (1880–1882)

    1881 George W. Van Slyke House, 756 Madison Ave.

c. 1881 Residence, 283 State St.

    1882 Albany County Bank Building, SE cor. of State St. and S. Pearl St., demolished 1927

Fuller and Wheeler (1883–1897)

    1883 Albany Safe Deposit and Storage Company Building, Maiden La. and Lodge St., demolished

c. 1885 Horace G. Young House, 425 State St.

1886–1887 YMCA Building, 60 N. Pearl St.

c. 1889 Edward McKinney House, 391 State St.

    1889 Harmanus Bleecker Hall, Washington Ave., burned 1940, demolished

    1890 School No. 10, Central Ave. and Perry St.

1890–1891 Fort Orange Club, alterations and additions, 110 Washington Ave.

1890–1892 Andrew S. Draper House, 129 S. Lake Ave.

    1891 Alden Chester House, 139 S. Lake Ave.

    1891 Fourth Precinct Police Station, 419 Madison Ave.

    1892 Visscher family vault, Albany Rural Cemetery, section 76

    1893 Bender Bacteriological Laboratory, 138 S. Lake Ave., demolished

    1893 Dudley Observatory, 140 S. Lake Ave., demolished

    1893 School No. 6, 105 Second St., demolished

    1893 School No. 24, Delaware Ave. and Madison Ave., demolished

1895–1896 Masonic Temple, NW cor. of Lodge St. and Maiden La.

1895–1896 Potts Memorial Rectory, St. Peter's Church, State St.

    1896 353 State St., alterations

    1896 Residence, 341 State St., rebuilt facade

    1896 Residence, 479 State St., alterations

    1896 Row houses, S. Lake Ave., facing Washington Park

pre-1897 DeGraaf Building, S. Pearl St. bet. Beaver St. and William St., demolished

Albany Institute of History and Art (detail), 125 Washington Avenue. Albany Institute of History & Art.

Albert W. Fuller, design for a residence. Albert W. Fuller, Artistic Homes *(Boston: J. R. Osgood and Company, 1882). New York State Library.*

pre-1897 Ridgefield Athletic Club (later Ridgefield Park)

pre-1897 Home Savings Bank Building, 13 N. Pearl St., demolished

Albert Fuller (1897–1900)

    1898–1899 Albany Hospital (original buildings of Albany Medical Center), New Scotland Ave.

    1898–1899 Centennial Hall, St. Mary's Church, SW cor. of Lodge St. and Pine St.

    1898 97–99 Spring St.

Fuller and Pitcher (1900–1909)

    c.1901 Charles Gibson and William J. Walker Houses, 415–419 State St.

    c.1901 James McCredie House, 403 State St.

    1901–1902 Albany Public Bath No. 1, 665 Broadway, demolished

    1902 School No. 12 (Old Albany High School Annex), cor. of Washington Ave. and Robin St.

pre-1903 Apartment houses, Central Ave. bet. Robin St. and Bradford St., demolished

pre-1903 Hudson River Telephone Co., cor. of Chapel St. and Maiden La., demolished

pre-1903 Railroad Branch, YMCA, Broadway, demolished

    c. 1905 Albany Garage Co., 28 Howard St., demolished

    1906 E. P. Gavit House, 2 Thurlow Terr., demolished

    1907 Albany Institute of History and Art, 125 Washington Ave.

after 1907 Albany Orphan Asylum, New Scotland Ave.

Fuller and Robinson (1910–1923)

    1912 One Forty State apartment building (later the Berkshire Hotel), 140 State St.

    1916–1917 Globe Warehouse Co., Dongan Ave.

    1917 School No. 19, 395 New Scotland Ave.

    c. 1920 Albany Hardware and Iron Co., cor. of Broadway and Arch St.

    c. 1920–1922 Park Branch, National Commercial Bank, 200 Washington Ave., enlargement and remodeling

    1923–1924 Harmanus Bleecker Library (with J. H. Johnson and George Gleim), SE cor. of Washington Ave. and Dove St.

    1924–1925 University Club, cor. of Washington Ave. and Dove St.

    1925 Gates Aufsessor House, 570 Providence St.

    1925 78–82 State St., demolished

Attributed to Fuller

    c. 1890 Albert Fuller House, 497 State St.

    1890 Row houses, 343–351 State St., demolished

pre-1898 Guild House and Choir House, St. Peter's Episcopal Church, State St.

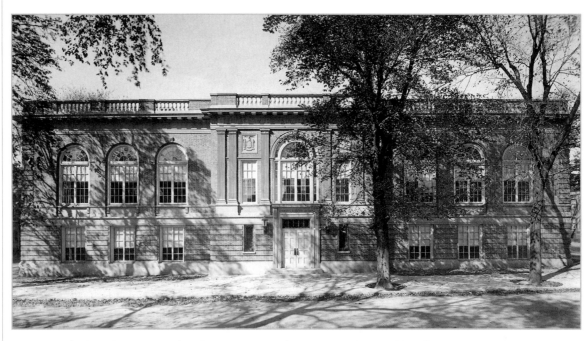

Harmanus Bleecker Library, corner of Washington Avenue and Dove Street. Albany Public Library.

Josiah Cleveland Cady

Cornelia Brooke Gilder

Albany's rusticated sandstone First Presbyterian Church, overlooking Washington Park at the corner of State and Willett streets, is typical of the powerful, dignified, but also welcoming Romanesque designs of New York City architect J. Cleveland Cady (1837–1919).

Born in Providence, Rhode Island, Cady graduated in 1860 from Trinity College in Hartford, Connecticut, where he later designed several buildings and ultimately bequeathed his architectural library and 20 albums of photographs.

Cady apprenticed in New York under a German architect and for a time with Alexander Jackson Davis. He established his own practice in 1870. His early High Victorian style is evident in the Oyster Bay Presbyterian Church on Long Island (1873), but in the next few years his style evolved from Gothic to the Romanesque. Trinity College's picturesque fraternity, St. Anthony's Hall (1878), combined a round turret with pointed arches and other Gothic features.

By the time he came to Albany, Cady was fully under the sway of Henry Hobson Richardson, and in Albany his new Presbyterian church was to be a neighbor of Richardson's Sard house on State Street, also begun in 1882. Norcross Brothers, Richardson's favored builder, constructed Cady's First Presbyterian Church. Many of his church exteriors show Richardsonian influence, with their arched entrance portals and massive, square corner towers, as seen at the Albany church but even more impressively at the First Presbyterian Church in Morristown, New Jersey. Cady's scores of church interiors were distinctively his own. A devout Presbyterian, Cady eschewed the nave of the Anglican and Catholic traditions in favor of an adaptable theater-like plan, more suitable for "low church" denominations. For large services, sliding doors could extend worship spaces into meeting spaces. In Albany the sanctuary of Cady's church is decorated with exceptional stained glass by the studios of J. and R. Lamb and Louis Tiffany.

While at work on Albany's First Presbyterian Church, Cady was also designing the first Metropolitan Opera House in New York. In the 1890s he began a grand plan for the Museum of Natural History. Only the south wing, facing West Seventy-seventh Street, was constructed, but that turreted and muscular landmark of pink granite ranks as one of New York City's great examples of the Romanesque revival.

Cady's imposing collegiate buildings are found throughout the Ivy League. At Yale he designed 15 structures, including Berkeley and Pierson colleges, the Sheffield Laboratory, Chittenden Library, and the law school. Throughout the 1880s and 1890s other Cady buildings went up on the campuses of Williams (Morgan Hall), Wesleyan (Fayerweather Gymnasium), and his alma mater, Trinity (Jarvis Hall of Science).

Philanthropy and architecture were entwined in Cady's life. He was a governor of Presbyterian Hospital and advised on its structural needs. He also designed a building for New York's Skin and Cancer Hospital, where he served as president of the board. For many years Cady worked in partnership with Charles I. Berg and Milton See.

Cady died in New York City at the age of 82, still planning Sunday school programs for the Church of the Covenant, where he served as Sunday school superintendent for 53 years.

Building List

1882 First Presbyterian Church of Albany, cor. of State St. and Willett St.

First Presbyterian Church of Albany, corner of State and Willett streets. Albany Institute of History & Art Library. Interior, Historic Albany Foundation.

Robert W. Gibson

Cornelia Brooke Gilder

Robert Williams Gibson (1854–1927) was a newly qualified, 27-year-old English architect when he arrived in Albany in 1881. He left seven years later for New York City a naturalized American and a recognized architectural figure. His design for Albany's Cathedral of All Saints had been chosen in competition with the eminent Henry Hobson Richardson, and the success of his National Commercial Bank building at 38 State Street had led to his first New York City commission, a building for the U.S. Trust Company on Wall Street. While only briefly a resident Albany architect, Robert Gibson launched his long and prominent American career in this city.

Born in England at Essex, the son of a wheelwright, Gibson began his architectural education in the army with the Royal Engineers. He went on to the Royal Academy of

National Commercial Bank, 38 State Street. The Industries of the City of Albany (Albany: Elstner Publishing Company, 1889). Albany Public Library.

Arts in 1875, where he won silver medals for architectural drawing in 1877 and 1878. At graduation he was awarded a traveling scholarship to study the great architecture of Spain, France, Germany, and Italy. Within a few years of immigrating to the United States, Gibson was designing his own cathedral in Albany. The cornerstone was laid in 1884.

In his first years in Albany Gibson worked as a partner of William Pretyman, an interior decorator and stained-glass designer. Gibson also designed two picturesque structures at the Albany Rural Cemetery, the lodge (1882) and chapel (1884), and two imposing houses on choice lots overlooking Washington Park on Englewood Place. Gibson worked in stone and brick and in his Albany years, through 1885, favored the Romanesque style. Later, when practicing in New York, he diversified into the Beaux-Arts and Colonial Revival styles for country houses, institutional buildings, hotels, and banks.

Religious structures, however, remained his specialty. He designed Episcopal churches all over New York State—in Rochester, Olean, Ossining, Gloversville, Corning, and Mechanicville, as well as in Plainfield, New Jersey, and Northampton, Massachusetts. He also redesigned the fire-gutted interior of Richard Upjohn's St. Paul's Episcopal Cathedral in Buffalo. Throughout his career Gibson kept returning to Albany to supervise further phases of his unfinished Cathedral of All Saints.

After moving to New York City, Robert Gibson married Caroline Hammond in 1890 and was well received in New York society. A member of the Seawanhaka Yacht Club, he designed their new clubhouse in Oyster Bay. He was a longtime member of the Century Association, a director of the American Institute of Architects, and two-term president of the Architectural League. In his retirement Gibson wrote a philosophical book, *The Morality of Nature*. He died in 1927 in Woodbury, Long Island, at Aveley Farm, the home he named after his Essex birthplace.

Albany Rural Cemetery, Lodge. George Roger Howell and Jonathon Tenney, History of Albany County, *vol. 2 (New York: W. W. Munsell and Company Publishers, 1886). Albany Institute of History & Art Library.*

Robert W. Gibson, design for Cathedral of All Saints. Albany Institute of History & Art.

Evans-Pruyn House, 7 Englewood Place. American Architect and Building News, *February 9, 1889.*

Building List

1882   Lodge, Albany Rural Cemetery
1884   Chapel, Albany Rural Cemetery
c. 1884   Evans-Pruyn House and Stables, 7 Englewood Pl., house demolished, carriage house remodeled
1884–1887, 1904   Cathedral of All Saints, cor. of Swan St. and Elk St.
1885   Craig House, 5 Englewood Pl.
1886   Pulpit, St. Peter's Church, State St.
1887   National Commercial Bank (later the Hampton Hotel), 38 State St.
1889   Monument for Mr. and Mrs. Amasa J. Parker, Albany Rural Cemetery

Cathedral of All Saints, corner of Swan and Elk streets. Photograph provided by M. McCarty and G. Gold.

Ernest Hoffman

Harold Colbeth

Ernest Hoffman, a prominent Albany architect of the late nineteenth century, was born on December 22, 1852, in Rome, New York. His family moved to Albany early in his childhood, and he was educated first in local public schools and later at the Albany Academy. His father, the Rev. Ernest Hoffman, was for 25 years pastor of the German-speaking St. John's Evangelical Lutheran Church on Central Avenue.

Upon graduation from the Albany Academy, Hoffman began his architectural career as an apprentice to Charles C. Nichols, then in partnership with J. B. Halcott in Albany. In 1877 Hoffman opened his own office at 9 North Pearl Street.

Hoffman's early work reflects the spirit of an age dominated by Henry Hobson Richardson and the Romanesque Revival. His rock-faced-granite Steamer No. 1 Firehouse and the LaDow house on Thurlow Terrace are both Richardsonian in their scale, stone polychromy (now obscured at the LaDow house but still evident at the firehouse), and their complex, pyramidal roof lines. Hoffman's delight in rich surface carving is evident in the sandstone trim on Steamer No. 1 and to an even greater extent on the front facade of the Scott Dumont Goodwin house at 333 State Street, which is reputed to be the work of stone carvers from the state Capitol.

By the early twentieth century Hoffman had made the transition to the Renaissance Revival as seen in the five-story Nusbaum and Livingston Building on Broadway, which is embellished with Corinthian pilasters. Like Marcus T. Reynolds and other turn-of-the century architects and builders in Albany, Hoffman also employed the Dutch Revival style. His downtown office building for the Albany Insurance Company had stepped gables on its two street facades.

Ernest Hoffman's career was not limited to Albany. He is known to have designed St. Alphonsus French Catholic Church in Glens Falls, St. Peter's Lutheran Church in Brooklyn, and several churches in Jersey City. Hoffman died on March 26, 1908. His last notable work is said to have been the Jermain house on Broadway in Menands.

Building List

c. 1882   Facade, Scott Dumont Goodwin House (with Franklin H. Janes), 333 State St.

1886   St. John's German Evangelical Lutheran Church, Central Ave.

1886   St. Matthew's First German Evangelical Lutheran Church, Delaware Ave. bet. Clinton Ave. and Elizabeth St., demolished

c. 1887   Residences, 37–45 S. Lake Ave. (number 39 was Ernest Hoffman's residence)

1889   Dobler Brewery, cor. of S. Swan St. and Myrtle Ave., demolished

1891   Charles LaDow House, 10 Thurlow Terr.

1892   Steamer No. 1 Firehouse, cor. of Washington Ave. and Western Ave.

Steamer No. 1 Firehouse, corner of Washington and Western avenues. Albany Institute of History & Art.

1898 Miller Merchandising Building, 48–50 S. Pearl St.

1902 Nusbaum and Livingston Building, 529–531 Broadway

pre-1903 Albany Insurance Company, 93 State St., 32–34 Lodge St., demolished 1966

pre-1903 Brown House, 724 Madison Ave., demolished

pre-1903 J. F. McElroy House, 131 S. Lake Ave.

pre-1903 Lewis J. Miller House, 305 Madison Ave., demolished

pre-1903 Railroad YMCA, Watervliet Ave., demolished

pre-1903 Row houses, 221–225 N. Pearl St.

J. F. McElroy House, 131 South Lake Avenue. Photograph by Joe Putrock.

Charles LaDow House, 10 Thurlow Terrace. Photograph by Joe Putrock.

Marcus T. Reynolds

Kenneth G. Reynolds Jr.

More than any other architect of his period, Marcus Reynolds (1869–1937) changed the face of downtown Albany. Among his dramatic structures in the heart of the city are the Albany Trust Company Building (1902, 1908, and 1930s); the United Traction Building (1899); the Albany City Savings Institution, said to be Albany's first skyscraper (1902 and 1924); and most of all the Delaware and Hudson Building and its attached Albany Evening Journal Building at the foot of State Street.

Although born in Great Barrington, Massachusetts, on August 20, 1869, Marcus Tullius Reynolds sprang from a long and distinguished line of Albanians and lived almost all his life in Albany at 98 Columbia Street. After attending the Albany Academy and St. Paul's School in Concord, New Hampshire, and graduating in 1890 from Williams College, Reynolds entered the architectural program at the School of Mines at Columbia University, where in 1893 his thesis was published as the prize essay of the American Economic Society. Entitled *Housing of the Poor in American Cities*, it is still cited in scholarly publications. The next two years he spent traveling and studying architecture throughout Europe, returning to America in October 1895.

For many years Reynolds was deeply interested in developing the then-decaying portion of the city lying south of State Street between Broadway and the Hudson River, and he made many surveys and drawings of this riverfront area. Eventually his proposals met with public approval and resulted in the plaza and the Delaware and Hudson Building and the Albany Evening Journal Building. Inspired by the Cloth Hall at Ypres, Belgium, the Flemish Gothic complex was completed in 1918. The exterior is embellished with bas reliefs redolent with images of early regional history: crouching beavers, the seals of the city and the state, and the coats of arms not only of Francis I of France, the States General of Holland, and the Duke of Albany but also of early Dutch families who settled the Hudson Valley. Panels under the windows of the Evening Journal Building depict the marks of famous European printers. Atop the tower is a replica, in copper, of the *Half Moon*.

Reynolds's designs consistently took advantage of prominent sites, often at corners, where he used such devices as domes and angled walls. His buildings—ranging from his earliest Renaissance Revival designs like the Van Rensselaer row houses (1897) to the Colonial Revival buildings late in his career, such as Hackett Junior High School (1927)—are richly detailed with such decorative elements as cartouches, swags, finials, pilasters, and pediments.

Reynolds's practice, although concentrated in Albany, had a regional impact. Banks were one of his specialties, and he designed bank buildings for Hudson, Catskill, and Amsterdam, New York. The Cooperstown railroad station (1915) was his work, as well as other buildings in Schenectady and Saratoga Springs.

A bachelor, Reynolds took his nephew, Kenneth Reynolds, into the practice in 1914. Marcus Reynolds

Van Rensselaer House, 389 State Street. Photograph provided by M. McCarty and G. Gold.

continued to handle large commissions until shortly before his death in 1937. These last works included a new building for his alma mater, the Albany Academy (1931), and the Gideon Putnam, the well-known Saratoga Springs hotel.

Building List

1893 Albany Terminal Storage Warehouse Co., Tivoli St.

1893 Van Rensselaer Manor House, part moved to Williamstown, Mass., later disassembled

1896–1897 Van Rensselaer Houses, 385–389 State St.

1898 Albany Country Club, remodeled and enlarged, Western Ave., demolished

1899–1900 Albany Railroad Co. (later United Traction Co.), 600 Broadway

1899 Curtis Douglas House, 4 Elk St., facade remodeled

1899 Garrit Yates Lansing House, 294 State St., alterations

1899 New York State Normal School Dormitory, proposal

1899 Superintendent's House, Albany Rural Cemetery, Menands

1900–1901 Pruyn Free Library, cor. of N. Pearl St. and Clinton Ave.; addition, 1926, demolished

1901 Meads Building, 545 Broadway

1901–1902 Albany City Savings Institution, 100 State St., east section

1901–1902 Canon George Carter House (now offices of the Cathedral of All Saints), 62 S. Swan St.

1901–1904 Van Rensselaer Apartments, cor. of Madison Ave. and Lark St.

1902 National Savings Bank, 70–72 State St., demolished

1902–1904 Albany Trust Co., 31-33 State St.; additions, 1908, 1930s

1902–1904 New York State National Bank, 69 State St.; addition, 1916, demolished

1903–1905 Ryder Apartments, 355 State St.

1904 Edmund Niles Huyck House, 319 State St.; addition, 1915

1904–1906 The Hampton, 40 State St., additions

1907–1908 First National Bank of Albany, 35–37 State St.

1907–1908 Homeopathic Hospital (later Memorial Hospital), 123 N. Pearl St.

1908 William Wallace House, 6 Elk St., facade remodeled

1909 William J. Barnes Bungalow (later SUNY Albany Chapel); 16 Waverly Pl., addition, 1912, burned

1910 Hampton Plaza café, alterations

Albany Trust Company, 31-33 State Street. Photograph provided by M. McCarty and G. Gold.

Truck House No. 4, corner of Delaware Avenue and Marshall Street. Photograph provided by M. McCarty and G. Gold.

Delaware and Hudson Building and Albany Evening Journal Building, Broadway at foot of State Street. Photograph provided by M. McCarty and G. Gold.

Municipal Gas Company, 126 State Street. Photograph provided by M. McCarty and G. Gold.

1910 Truck House No. 4, NE cor. of Delaware Ave. and Marshall St.

1912–1918 Delaware and Hudson Building and Albany Evening Journal Building, Broadway at foot of State St.

1913–1915 Albany Industrial Building, 1031 Broadway

1915 Harmon Pumpelly Read House, 7 Elk St., facade remodeled

1915–1916 Municipal Gas Co., 126 State St.

1922–1924 Public School No. 4, cor. of Madison Ave. and Ontario St., demolished

1924 Albany City Savings Institution, 100 State St., center and west sections

1925–1927 William S. Hackett Junior High School, 45 Delaware Ave.

1928–1931 Albany Academy, Academy Rd.

1930 Albany Academy (Joseph Henry Memorial), Academy Park, cupola reconstructed; alterations, 1935

Shepley, Rutan & Coolidge

Cornelia Brooke Gilder

In March 1886, as he lay dying, 47-year-old Henry Hobson Richardson directed his three top architectural assistants to carry out the firm's unfinished work. Two of them—George Foster Shepley (1860–1903), engaged at the time to Richardson's daughter Julia, and Charles Hercules Rutan (1851–1914), a longtime engineering specialist who had joined the firm as an office boy—had been supervising far-flung office projects for some time. The third, a talented designer named Charles Allerton Coolidge (1858–1936), had in recent years risen to become Richardson's "favorite."

The new firm, Shepley, Rutan and Coolidge, soon became national in scope, with branch offices in St. Louis (Shepley's hometown) and Chicago. The partners were best known for their commercial, academic, and civic buildings. They continued at first to work in the Romanesque style while completing the projects of their larger-than-life mentor, including the Allegheny County Courthouse in Pittsburgh and Stanford University. The new firm's first two railroad stations, in Hartford and Springfield, both built in 1889, reflect their Richardsonian legacy.

Albany's turn-of-the-century Union Station belongs to a later, Beaux-Arts era. Its trio of entrance portals on the street and track facades, however, recalls the triple arches of Richardson's Albany City Hall. (Shepley and Rutan had been employed by Richardson in the early 1880s when the city hall was constructed.) In 1899 and 1900, while working on Albany's station, Shepley, Rutan and Coolidge had two imposing depots under construction in Boston. South Station (1899), a four-story corner landmark, still survives. North Station (1900), now demolished, was a one-story structure entered through a massive triumphal arch.

Shepley, Rutan and Coolidge's Boston offices were in the top floor of one of their early commercial structures, the Ames Building (1892). They designed numerous buildings for Harvard, from the gracious brick dormitories along the Charles River in Cambridge (now part of Winthrop and Kirkland Houses) to the marmoreal, Classical Revival medical school in downtown Boston. Other academic commissions were the chapel at Vassar College and the John Hay Library at Brown. Like Richardson, the firm apparently did no work in New York City, but in the Midwest they designed several important structures, including the Art Institute of Chicago and the public library and commercial buildings in St. Louis.

Shepley died unexpectedly on vacation in Switzerland in 1903, and Rutan in 1914. Coolidge continued the practice, bringing in his partner's son, Henry Richardson

Shepley, as well as Francis V. Bulfinch and Lewis Abbott. They designed more Harvard buildings—the neo-Georgian Fogg Art Museum (1925–1927) and the biological laboratories, considered Harvard's first "modern" building. Charles Coolidge also specialized in hospital design and late in life traveled to such distant places as Beijing and Istanbul with plans for modern hospitals.

Building List

1899–1900   Union Station, 575 Broadway

Union Station, 575 Broadway. Photograph provided by M. McCarty and G. Gold.

Union Station, interior. Albany Institute of History & Art.

York & Sawyer

Cornelia Brooke Gilder

Monumentality, security, and confidence—these were the hallmarks of the buildings of the noted New York architectural firm of York and Sawyer. One of the firm's earliest bank commissions, National Commercial Bank (1901–1903) at 60 State Street in Albany, exemplifies these trademarks. This classical "temple of fortune," with an imposing Ionic portico and marble-faced interior, resembles two other early works by the architects: the Starr Library at Middlebury College (1900) in Vermont and the Riggs National Bank (1902) on Pennsylvania Avenue in Washington, D.C.

Having trained with McKim, Mead and White, Edward York (1865–1928) and Philip Sawyer (1868–1949) were in their thirties when they formed their own partnership in 1898. In McKim, Mead and White's office they had been given charge of residential commissions, but in their own practice they would be known for institutional and commercial structures. At the peak of their careers in the prosperous 1920s, York and Sawyer designed a series of impressive banks in Manhattan, including one of the country's key financial institutions, the Federal Reserve of New York (1924), a mighty Florentine palazzo with five levels of underground vaults, and the midtown Bowery Savings Bank (1923), with its richly appointed Romanesque banking room. Conveniently located opposite Grand Central Terminal, the Bowery Savings Bank building was a prime midtown location. York and Sawyer moved their architectural offices there in 1924.

Outside New York City York and Sawyer designed many banks, including the Royal Bank of Canada in Montreal (1928), hospitals, and academic buildings, particularly on the campuses of Middlebury and Vassar, as well as a grand Gothic law library at the University of Michigan (1922–1923). In Washington, D.C., York and Sawyer were well known in the corridors of power. As bank experts, they were commissioned to survey conditions of the Department of the Treasury building in 1909. Their report led to years of work modernizing and enlarging that building. Over a 20-year period, between 1913 and 1932, they designed and constructed the Department of Commerce building. Edward York died before that building was completed, but Sawyer carried on the practice through the 1930s with Louis Ayres, a colleague from McKim, Mead and White's office, whom York and Sawyer had made a partner in 1910.

National Commercial Bank, 60 State Street. Photograph provided by M. McCarty and G. Gold.

Building List

1901–1903   National Commercial Bank (currently Key Bank), 60 State St.

McKim, Mead & White

Cornelia Brooke Gilder

By 1900 McKim, Mead and White's elegant townhouses graced fashionable residential districts in many American cities, usually on conspicuous corner sites. Some early ones were Romanesque—the Ross Winans house in Baltimore (1882) and the Louis C. Tiffany house in New York (1882–1885). But after their extraordinary block-long Villard Houses in New York (1881–1885), the Florentine palazzo became the firm's most popular urban style. Some memorable examples are the Patterson house, with its butterfly-shaped plan, on Dupont Circle in Washington, D.C. (1900), and the H. H. Cook house and the Payne Whitney house on Fifth Avenue in New York (1906), where the current owner, the Cultural Services Division of the French Embassy, has recently restored the magnificent, mirrored Venetian Room.

In contrast to these Old World palaces, Albany's Arnold house, on the corner of State Street and Sprague Place (1902–1904), is a dignified red-brick Colonial house that belongs on Boston's Beacon Hill. It is reminiscent of the old Beacon Street house designed by Asher Benjamin where McKim set up a temporary office while working on the Boston Public Library in 1887.

Set back behind an iron fence and elevated on a high stone basement, the Arnold house looks both important and discreet. Bow-shaped bays flank the graceful Classical portico, which is supported by paired Ionic columns. Over the first-floor windows carved marble lintels rest on consoles; the smooth upper-story lintels have keystones and splayed ends. These careful details, as well as the wrought-iron balconies with a delicate quarter-circle pattern and the balustrade above the cornice, were all features of other McKim, Mead and White neo-Federal townhouses in New York City: the James Junius Goodwin house (1898), the Charles Dana Gibson house (1903), and the Percy Pyne house (1906–1912).

By the time the Arnold house was under construction, McKim, Mead and White was well established as America's leading architectural firm. Over its 20-year history the firm had supervised hundreds of public and private projects and had become a veritable architectural school. Many architects moved on to establish independent, prominent practices after working on the staff, which at its peak numbered 100 employees.

Many McKim, Mead and White buildings have been demolished in the course of the twentieth century. In Albany, however, the Arnold house, representing the mature work of Stanford White, and the Senate Chamber in the New York State Capitol, where White worked as a young man under Henry Hobson Richardson, both remain cherished features of the fabric of the city. The Arnold

house has been owned for many years by the Roman Catholic Diocese of Albany and at times has served as the bishop's residence.

Building List

1902–1904 Benjamin Arnold House, cor. of State St. and Sprague Pl. Carriage house, 307 Washington Ave.

Benjamin Arnold House, corner of State Street and Sprague Place. Photograph provided by M. McCarty and G. Gold.

Worthington Palmer

Erin M. Tobin

Albany architect and real-estate broker Worthington Palmer (1878–1940) started his career in the office of Marcus T. Reynolds. Born in Albany in May 1878, Palmer graduated from Albany Academy in 1895 and from the Massachusetts Institute of Technology in 1899. From MIT Palmer moved to Buffalo, where he worked for a short period of time. Palmer had returned to Albany by 1905, living with his parents, Edward DeLancey Palmer and Sarah Worthington Palmer, and his brother DeLancey Palmer.

Once in Albany Worthington Palmer worked as a draftsman in Reynolds's office, where he contributed to the design of several buildings, including early work on the Delaware and Hudson Building on Broadway in Albany. Palmer received one of his first commissions from his step-grandmother, Martha Palmer, the widow of Amos Palmer, for a house at 371 State Street. *American Architect and Building News* published an image of this house, completed in 1906, in its January 12, 1907, issue. Palmer designed 371 State Street in the neoclassical style, typified by a roofline balustrade, dentiled cornice, and broken pediment over the arched entrance.

After his father passed away, Worthington Palmer began working with his brother DeLancey Palmer at the Edward DeLancey Palmer Company, a real-estate and insurance agency. Worthington Palmer was working in this office by 1913. When he returned from serving in World War I, he entered his most prolific phase as an independent architect. He designed many alterations or additions to existing structures, as at 54 Willett Street (1920) and 151 South Lake Avenue (1921). The house at 54 Willett Street, where Palmer designed the brickwork, new entry, and steps, shares some similarities to his design of 371 State Street, including the prominent flat marble lintels with distinctive projecting voussoirs above the 12-over-1 windows. On Willett Street this detail has an Art Deco feel, contrasted with the neoclassical stylized lintels at 371 State Street.

In the mid-1920s Palmer won commissions for several new buildings, including a house built for Charles Ruffner, vice president of Adirondack Power and Light Corporation, at 2125 Rosendale Road in Niskayuna (1924). This house, sited on a rise overlooking Rosendale Road, originally had three elevations visible from the road, two of which can no longer be seen from a public right-of-way due to vegetation growth and other residential construction surrounding the property. Palmer also designed the clubhouse for the Schuyler Meadows Country Club, on Schuyler Meadows Road in Loudonville, in 1926.

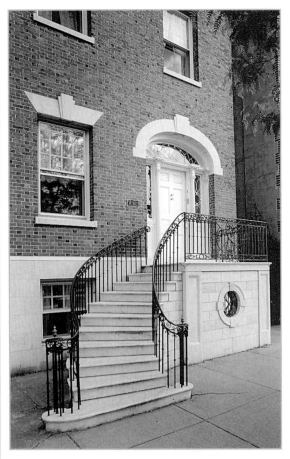

54 Willett Street. Photograph provided by M. McCarty and G. Gold.

The 1934 Albany city directory lists Worthington Palmer as an architect residing at the Fort Orange Club, 110 Washington Avenue. In 1929 Palmer designed a new athletic wing and oversaw alterations to the east wall and added neoclassical elements to the front facade of this prestigious club, following the style he used throughout his career. In 1937 he remodeled the club's tap room into a handsome space. Worthington Palmer passed away on July 2, 1940.

Building List

1906   371 State St.
1920   54 Willett St., new facade and entry steps
1921   151 S. Lake Ave., rear addition, altered
1929   Fort Orange Club, 110 Washington Ave., addition and alterations
1937   Fort Orange Club, 110 Washington Ave., remodeling of tap room

371 State Street. Photograph provided by M. McCarty and G. Gold.

George L. Heins and Albert Randolph Ross

Cornelia Brooke Gilder

Nothing in the serene, orderly exteriors of three classical brick buildings of the *Downtown Campus of the University at Albany, on Western Avenue at Robin Street, reveals the aesthetic controversy and political power play embedded in their history. A young outsider in private practice, Albert Randolph Ross (1868–1948), challenged the official state architect, George Lewis Heins (1860–1907), with alternative designs for this trio of connected structures, known as Hawley, Husted, and Draper halls.*

The key figure in the construction of the campus was neither of the architects but the formidable commissioner of education, Dr. Andrew Sloan Draper, a man known by some as a conscientious and intelligent visionary and by others as an impatient bully who would even take advantage of a vacationing bishop in a land grab for the State Education Building. Trained as a lawyer and experienced in state government as a Republican assemblyman, Draper had recently returned to Albany after leading a successful building campaign at the University of Illinois.

On a frosty January evening in 1906 from his front porch on South Lake Avenue, Draper saw flames rising from the hulking, cramped State Normal School on Willett Street. It was a building he had always considered "ill-favored and ill-fated," and he later recollected dryly that his "personal grief was not uncontrollable." For the future teachers of New York State, Draper wanted a commodious, classical campus. The elm-shaded grounds of the former Albany Orphan Asylum were the perfect site, and he asked George Heins, as the state architect, to design three connected structures.

Born in Philadelphia, Heins had met his future architectural partner, Christopher Grant LaFarge, son of the stained-glass artist John LaFarge, during their student days at Massachusetts Institute of Technology. They went into practice together in New York City in 1886, and soon afterward Heins married his partner's aunt, Aimée LaFarge.

Only two years into their practice the young architects won the prestigious commission for the Cathedral of St. John the Divine in New York City (though Heins lived to see only the choir of this vast church completed). Meanwhile, the firm designed and finished many churches and even two other cathedrals. In 1899 Governor Theodore Roosevelt had appointed Heins as state architect, and

Heins's world became split between his office with LaFarge in Manhattan and his state office at the Capitol, near his home at 303 State Street and his club, the Fort Orange.

With LaFarge as principal designer and Heins commuting from Albany to run the business and oversee construction, the firm often worked in Byzantine and Romanesque styles. It also pioneered the use of new technology, like the Guastavino vault, and integrated imaginative decorative features. Between 1900 and 1904 they ornamented stops on the New York City subway system with visually distinctive and colorfully glazed terracotta plaques to orient the traveler. Above ground, their 133 metal-and-glass Beaux-Arts-style subway entrance kiosks graced the city streets.

Heins and LaFarge designed other grand Beaux-Arts structures for exotic animals, from egrets to elephants, at the New York Zoological Garden (now the Bronx Zoo), a pet project of Governor Roosevelt. In 1905, soon after Roosevelt's election to a second presidential term, the firm also produced a new reception room at his country house, Sagamore Hill, overlooking Oyster Bay.

The growth of state government multiplied Heins's workload in Albany. Within the massive but already inadequate Capitol, he installed mezzanines for more offices, improved circulation, and addressed structural problems. He oversaw the construction or renovation of a host of buildings across the state—from armories to asylums, Indian schools, and buildings on the Cornell University campus.

The plans for the State Normal College in Albany got off to a slow start. Heins produced rough sketches in March 1906, provisional drawings in June, and final plans in August—none of which survive today. But records indicate that Draper was not impressed. The buildings Heins presented were, in Draper's eyes, a provincial Dutch design, sited in a way that would require removal of century-old elms.

Meanwhile, a new architect, Albert Randolph Ross —trained in the offices of McKim, Mead and White and clutching a portfolio of photographs of the new Jeffersonian buildings at the University of Virginia— offered Draper the campus he had visualized.

Working on speculation, Ross produced preliminary sketches in just two weeks and soon had final designs. Draper asked Heins to accept Ross's plans and work with him on the interiors. Heins refused, claiming that Ross's grand classical porticos would exceed the budget and that under state law he was not authorized to employ a private architect.

The battle over the college buildings went to the state Legislature and even into the national press. The *American Architect and Building News* supported Draper: "the architectural work of the state cannot be done efficiently, promptly and economically by a single public official, no matter how able or how adequately paid." Heins conceded to Draper in March 1907 and on a New York City-bound train worked out financial details with Ross. Heins never lived to see the completed college.

In September 1907 the 47-year-old Heins died at his country house at Mohegan Lake, New York. Officially his death was listed as a case of meningitis, but the *New York Times* reported that the overworked architect had suffered a nervous breakdown. (In 1908 the Legislature appointed a deputy to assist his successor.)

Who was the handsome, persuasive interloper, Albert Randolph Ross? Eight years younger than Heins, Ross had apprenticed with his architect father in Iowa and by the age of 23 had worked his way from Davenport into the New York City offices of McKim, Mead and White. Maintaining his valuable ties with this leading firm, Ross

opened his own office in 1897 and became a specialist in neoclassical libraries.

Ross's 1906 design for the State Normal College made the buildings teaching tools themselves, exhibiting the spectrum of Greek orders—Corinthian, Doric, and Ionic—in their porticos. Here was the inspiring school for teachers Draper wanted. Twenty-five years later Ross wrote, "I tried to reflect the refinement of the Italian Renaissance in the treatment of detail, and with the tapestry brick walls, the ivory terra-cotta and lime-stone shafts."

As tastes for traditional architecture waned, Ross's classicism would be his downfall. His last grandiose building, the Milwaukee County Courthouse of 1931, with towering Corinthian colonnades and vast arches, was sneered at by Frank Lloyd Wright as Ross's "million dollar rockpile." Wright predicted that "the new courthouse will set Milwaukee back fifty years from any cultural standpoint."

Ross died in 1948 in his favorite place, a bungalow on Boothbay Harbor, Maine, which he and his wife, Susan Husted, had built in 1908, the year after his triumph with Andrew Draper and the State Normal College at Albany.

Building List

1906–1908 Hawley Hall, Husted Hall, and Draper Hall, State Normal College (later the New York State College for Teachers at Albany, now the Downtown Campus of the University at Albany, State University of New York)

Husted Hall, Draper Hall, and Hawley Hall, State Normal College (now the Downtown Campus of the University at Albany, State University of New York). M. E. Grenander Department of Special Collections and Archives, University at Albany Libraries.

Palmer & Hornbostel

Cornelia Brooke Gilder

The New York State Education Building, Albany's heroically proportioned Greek temple facing the New York State Capitol, was designed by Henry Hornbostel (1867–1961) and by George Carnegie Palmer (1862–1934) at the peak of their architectural careers.

New York architect, bridge builder, and educator Hornbostel first worked with his future partner Palmer as a young intern in 1891 after graduating from Columbia University. Hornbostel went on to study in Paris at the École des Beaux-Arts and to work for the architectural firm of Girault and Blavette.

Back in New York in 1897 Hornbostel worked as a freelance delineator for some of the city's top architectural firms, including McKim, Mead and White; Howell and Stokes; and Carrère and Hastings. Hornbostel's magisterial designs and skilled perspective drawings led to success in nationwide architectural competitions, first when he was an employee at established firms and later when he was a partner with his former boss George Palmer, who was also a Columbia graduate.

Working together for more than 20 years, from 1899 to 1921, Palmer and Hornbostel specialized in civic and academic buildings, as well as bridges. Their best-known college campuses are Carnegie Mellon University (1904) in Pittsburgh and Emory University (1915) in Atlanta. In a single year, 1910, they had four major city halls under design and construction: in Hartford, Connecticut; Wilmington, Delaware; Pittsburgh, Pennsylvania; and Oakland, California. Among their bridge commissions were the Williamsburg and Queensboro bridges (1905) and the Hell Gate railroad bridge (1917), all in New York City. In addition to his architectural practice, Hornbostel was dedicated to the instruction of young architects. In Pittsburgh he founded the architecture school at Carnegie Mellon and served as its first director and in New York City lectured at Columbia University.

In 1907 Palmer and Hornbostel won the competition for the New York State Education Building in Albany. This vast temple, with its exterior design derived from

New York State Education Building, 89 Washington Avenue. Photograph provided by M. McCarty and G. Gold.

reconstructions of the exterior from the Tomb of Mausolus at Halicarnassus in Turkey, combines ancient architectural idioms with modern materials. The huge exterior columns were constructed with steel shafts clad with marble and surmounted by terra-cotta Corinthian capitals. The rectilinear exterior gives no hint of the dramatic rounded spaces within—a sky-lit neo-Roman rotunda of Indiana limestone, barrel-vaulted corridors, and a soaring reading room. This 30-foot-high space, spanned by Guastavino vaults, was inspired by the Bibliothèque Nationale de France, where Hornbostel had studied during his Paris days.

The imposing colonnaded exteriors of the Soldiers and Sailors Memorial in Pittsburgh (1909–1910) and an unexecuted library for Emory University in Atlanta (1915) are two of the firm's other designs that bear a close kinship to the New York State Education Building.

Palmer and Hornbostel's private houses—like Driftwood Manor (1906–1908, demolished 1980) in Riverhead, New York, and the Arthur S. Dwight house (1915) in Great Neck, New York—incorporate elliptical and circular rooms in their plans and exhibit a variety of styles from Mediterranean to Tudor. In Atlanta the firm designed a Tudor house for Coca-Cola magnate Charles Howard Chandler and laid out the campus for Emory University on an Italian Renaissance paradigm.

Sullivan Jones became a partner with Palmer and Hornbostel for about four years beginning in 1910. Hornbostel, in his forties, left to serve in World War I as a gas officer in Argonne, France. After his return the partnership ended. Palmer, a leading citizen of Morristown, New Jersey, continued to practice in New York City. Hornbostel long outlived Palmer. He was last employed as director of the Allegheny County park system in Pittsburgh, a city graced by many of the grandest structures of his notable career.

Building List

1907–1912 New York State Education Building, 89 Washington Ave.

New York State Education Building, New York State Library reading room. New York State Library.

Walter Hunter Van Guysling

William J. Higgins

Walter Hunter Van Guysling is an imaginative, versatile, yet rather elusive figure in Albany's early twentieth-century architectural history. His designs ranged from schools and commercial buildings to restaurants and government facilities, but he was also a residential architect whose houses combined grace with hints of whimsy. Born in Albany on September 23, 1878, Van Guysling began his training in 1894 as a draftsman under Isaac Perry, then the architect of the New York State Capitol. Later he worked under Marcus T. Reynolds, from 1899 to 1902, and Charles Ogden, beginning in 1904. Van Guysling's apprenticeship had clearly ended by 1909, when he became a partner in the short-lived firm of Ogden and Van Guysling. After a brief partnership with Dakin Judson in 1910, Van Guysling maintained his own practice in Albany until his untimely death in 1927.

Van Guysling was an excellent architectural renderer, with a delicate and fanciful style in ink and watercolor. During his association with Ogden, the office designed two buildings that sucessfully translated Van Guysling's airy rendering style into three dimensions: the Hudson River

R. B. Wing building, 384–386 Broadway. Courtesy of John G. Waite Associates, Architects.

Day Line ticket office (1907) on Broadway and Keeler's Restaurant (c. 1907) on State Street. In the following year his hand is also evident in the house built for Dr. Joseph Ivimey Dowling at 116 Washington Avenue (1908), with its curious stucco facades and diminutive, highly finished interiors.

Among the buildings Van Guysling designed in his own practice are the facade and renovation of the R. B. Wing building (1913–1914) on Broadway, the Amsterdam Apartments (1915) on Chestnut Street, and the small townhouse at 366 Hudson Avenue (1926–1927). In 1910 construction began on Van Guysling's designs for ten Colonial-style houses in a planned development known as Colonial Court Estates in Menands. These buildings included the Claude C. Nuckols House, 1 Kenmar Road (1910); Ann Elizabeth Jackson House, 2 South Lyons Avenue (1914); George E. Willcomb House, 14 Upland Road (1914); Sawyer House, 15 South Lyons Avenue (1915); Merritt E. Brown House, 20 Upland Road (1916); Ross Sims House, 30 Brookside Avenue (1919–1920); Emma M. Smith House, 3 Kenmar Road (1922–1923); and 11 and 17 South Lyons Avenue (1910–1923). Number 10 South Lyons Avenue was designed by Van Guysling as his family residence; he and his wife Grace resided there from its completion in 1913 until his death in 1927. Several other houses in Albany, Menands, and Loudonville are attributed to Van Guysling.

Though most of Van Guysling's extant buildings are in the Colonial Revival style, his work showed an eclecticism typical of its time, encompassing idioms from the formal Beaux-Arts classicism of the police station on North Pearl Street (1906) to the half-timbered romanticism of Keeler's. Some of Van Guysling's most distinctive and evocative Albany buildings show the combined influence of the Arts and Crafts and the Dutch Revival styles. His work is full of lively, imaginative references to Albany's Dutch past. A playful image of the early Dutch city emerges in details like the Flemish gables, ornamental ironwork, and complex casement windows of the Hudson River Day Line office and in the R. B. Wing store's stylized Hudson River sloops and prominent center dormer with projecting hoist beam. Van Guysling's lighthearted interpretations of Dutch architecture contrast with more serious, archeologically correct Dutch Revival essays like Marcus Reynolds's Pruyn Library, but they represent a significant chapter in Albany's long-standing architectural fascination with its Dutch heritage.

The Arts and Crafts spirit was most evident in the Joseph Ivimey Dowling house, with its rough-textured stucco facades and its superb fireplaces, stair railings, and other interior finishes in oak, tile, hammered copper, and leaded glass. The Arts and Crafts influence is less distilled but still evident in many of Van Guysling's Colonial Revival houses and even in the stucco facades of the R. B. Wing and Hudson River Day Line buildings.

Van Guysling's stylistic versatility and his eclectic sensibility were not unusual for their time. His free and flexible borrowings from the architecture of many eras and places were typical of his colleagues in Albany and beyond. Yet each of Van Guysling's buildings includes small twists of form and detail that mark it as the product of a distinctive view of design and history, and the work of a very individualistic architect.

Building List

Walter Hunter Van Guysling

 1906 Third Precinct Police Station, 222 N. Pearl St.

c. 1907 Keeler's Restaurant (with Charles Ogden), 56 State St., demolished

 1907 Hudson River Day Line Ticket Office (with Charles Ogden), 351 Broadway

 1908 Dr. Joseph Ivimey Dowling House (with Charles Ogden), 116 Washington Ave., demolished 1982

1913–1914 R. B. Wing Building, 384–386 Broadway, alterations

c. 1915 Public School No. 14 (now Philip Schuyler High School), 69 Trinity Pl.

 1915 Amsterdam Apartments, 2–6 Chestnut St., demolished

1926–1927 Residence, 366 Hudson Ave., alterations

Attributed to Walter Hunter Van Guysling

 1909 John S. Hoy House, 309 State St.

 1914 Edwin S. Bramley House, 125 S. Pine St.

 1914 Jasper Redmond House, 127 S. Pine St.

 1917 Keeler's Café, 3 Green St.

Public School No. 14, 69 Trinity Place. Portfolio of Construction Work by Morris Kantrowitz (Albany). Courtesy of Douglas Bucher.

Hudson River Day Line Ticket Office (detail), 351 Broadway. Albany Institute of History & Art Library.

Hoppin & Koen

Cornelia Brooke Gilder

The New York architectural firm of Hoppin and Koen is best remembered for their elegant country houses on the cliffs of Newport, beside shady country roads of Lenox, along the Hudson River, and on Long Island's North Shore. But in Albany their work is represented by a rare public building, the Albany County Courthouse (1914), in the civic heart of Capitol Hill.

One of the firm's most exacting clients, the articulate Edith Wharton, described her house, The Mount, as "spacious and dignified." These words equally depict the granite- and limestone-faced neoclassical courthouse building in Albany. Its design pays homage to its older neighbor, the New York State Court of Appeals (Henry Rector, 1835–1842). Hoppin designed a two-story engaged Ionic colonnade on the upper stories of the front and rear facades, which reflect Rector's grand Ionic portico on the older Greek Revival courthouse.

Born in Providence, Rhode Island, Francis Hoppin's (1867–1941) early architectural career alternated between travel and study abroad and apprenticeships at home, first with his architect brother, Howard, in Providence and after 1886 with the growing firm of McKim, Mead and White in New York City. Their busy office appreciated Hoppin's skill as a renderer. A co-worker at the firm described his evocative perspective drawings, which often depicted a proposed structure amidst "blue sky and trees

where there aren't any, flying shadows on the building, you know, a real snappy piece of work."

In 1894 Hoppin and an office mate, Terence Koen (1858–1923), established their own practice. The genial, suave, and socially connected Hoppin (soon to become a colonel in the Spanish-American War) was the more conspicuous partner, but he was evidently dependent on Koen. After his partner's death in 1923, Hoppin closed their midtown New York office, off Fifth Avenue on Forty-third Street.

Hoppin's Beaux-Arts training is evident in ornate town houses for such clients as James Lanier but is apparent more dramatically in the New York City Police Headquarters at 240 Centre Street (1909). This monumental domed structure, constrained on a triangular lot, was designed "to impress both the officer and prisoner with the majesty of the law." Beginning with Engine House No. 65 (1897) on Times Square, the firm designed a series of firehouses, police stations, theaters, and community buildings and secured the Albany County Courthouse commission through an architectural competition. While working on the courthouse, Hoppin was also remodeling Springwood, the Roosevelt country house at Hyde Park, for Sara Roosevelt, mother of future president Franklin Delano Roosevelt.

When World War I temporarily slowed down business, Hoppin took up watercolor painting. Retiring to Newport in the 1920s, he became well known for his exquisite architectural landscapes of familiar American resorts—Bar Harbor, Palm Beach, and Newport—as well as European scenes. He lived in a house once owned by Edith Wharton, sketched in a studio of his own design, and umpired tennis matches at the Casino. Hoppin outlived one of his Newport buildings, the central pavilion of Bailey's Beach Club, which was swept off its foundations in a hurricane in 1938, three years before his own death.

Building List

1914 Albany County Courthouse, cor. of Eagle St. and Columbia St.

Albany County Courthouse, corner of Eagle and Columbia streets. Albany Institute of History & Art.

Gander, Gander & Gander

John A. Gander

Albany carpenter Anton A. Gander had six sons who survived infancy. One became an electrician, two became contractors, and three—Joseph J. (1884–1967), Conrad J. (1890–1967), and John P. (1892–1973)—chose to be architects. Together, the Gander family has made a unique contribution to the building fabric of twentieth-century Albany.

In their early teens the brothers worked in their father's carpentry shop located behind their home at 63 Delaware Street. Two of the future architects, Joseph and Conrad, attended Columbia University and Provot's Atelier in New York City. Joseph went on to work for a prominent New York City architectural firm, Delano and Aldrich. Conrad, winner of the second medal in the Beaux-Arts National Competition in 1913 while still a student, started his career in the firm of Harry Allen Jacobs of New York City. The youngest of the three architect brothers, John P., attended Carnegie Institute of Technology before returning to Albany to practice with the well-known local architect Charles Ogden. Joseph and Conrad joined the firm shortly afterwards. Ogden and Gander's first commission, won through a competition in 1916, was the alteration of the interior of Albany City Hall. In their ten years with Charles Ogden, the Gander brothers established a solid reputation for institutional buildings: monasteries, convents, schools, and churches became a specialty of the firm.

The U.S. Post Office and Courthouse on Broadway (1931–1934) is the most noteworthy Albany commission of Gander, Gander and Gander. Designed in a neoclassical but modern style favored by the U.S. government in the 1930s, the monumental marble-faced facade is a good example of architecture coordinated with highly skilled craftsmanship—sculpture, friezes, and aluminum grillwork. The firm's subsequent buildings were less ornamental, as is typical of the mid-twentieth century, and employed contemporary materials and technology. Two major commissions—the Mater Christi Seminary and the New York State Health Department Building—date from the 1950s. Many of Gander, Gander and Gander's commissions were located on the fringes of the city,

U.S. Post Office and Courthouse, corner of Broadway and Maiden Lane. Photograph provided by M. McCarty and G. Gold.

reflecting the city's decentralized development during the firm's most productive period, from the 1920s through the 1950s.

Gander, Gander and Gander's practice was centered mainly in New York State, but the firm also completed commissions for religious institutions in Carey, Ohio; New Haven, Connecticut; and Washington, D.C. In 1942–1943 the firm made bold proposals for six major projects for the rejuvenation of Albany. Although not actually realized, these proposals included a new governor's mansion and a "victory mall" along the Hudson River.

Building List

Gander, Gander and Gander (through 1956)
1916 Albany City Hall, interior (with Charles Ogden), 24 Eagle St.
1916 Our Lady of Angels Convent, Sheridan Ave.
1920 Commerce Insurance Co., 42 Howard St.
1920 Farnham's Restaurant, 61 State St. and 5 James St., demolished
1924 House of Good Shepherd Sisters' Convent (now St. Anne's Institute), 25 W. Lawrence St.
1924 Sisters' Convent, St. Casimer's Parish, 317 Sheridan Ave.
1925 Newman Club, 741 Madison Ave.
1925 Tower, Our Lady Help of Christians Church, 66 Second Ave.
1926 Masterson Day Nursery, St. Charles Lwanga House, 115 Grand St.
1927 Mother House, Sisters of Mercy, 634 New Scotland Ave.

1928 Monastery of the Immaculate Conception (now part of Maria College), New Scotland Ave.
1931 Hall Realty Office Building, State St.
1931–1934 U.S. Post Office and Courthouse (with Electus D. Litchfield and Norman R. Sturgis), cor. of Broadway and Maiden La.
1933 American Legion Post No. 30, New Scotland Ave. near S. Lake Ave., demolished
1934 Dobler Brewery, cor. of Myrtle Ave. and S. Swan St., demolished
1934 Our Lady Help of Christians School, Second Ave. near Krank St.
1936 Louis DeRusso House, 106 S. Manning Blvd.
1936 Sisters' Convent, St. Mary's Roman Catholic Church, Pine St.
1936 Sisters of St. Francis Convent, 74 Second Ave.
1937 Commercial building (later Rudolph Brothers jewelry store), SE cor. of Pearl St. and State St., demolished
1941 Shapiro's Jewelry Store, 72 N. Pearl St., demolished
1942 West End Federal Savings and Loan Association, 854 Madison Ave.
1945 Singer Sewing Machine Co., 72 N. Pearl St., demolished
1945 Bridge over James St., John G. Myers Department Store, 37–41 N. Pearl St., demolished
1952 Mater Christi Seminary, cor. of New Scotland Ave. and McCormack Rd.
1953 New York State Health Department Building, 84 Holland Ave.
1955 Cardinal McCloskey High School, 106 Elm St., demolished
1956 Sisters' Convent, Cardinal McCloskey High School, Elm St., demolished

U.S. Post Office and Courthouse, Courtroom. Albany Institute of History & Art Library.

Sullivan W. Jones

William Brandow

Of all the architects discussed in this book Sullivan W. Jones (1878–1955) may have been the most politically connected, serving as a member of Gov. Alfred E. Smith's cabinet while he was state architect from 1923 to 1928. It was not Jones's official position with the State, however, that gave him a place in the cabinet, but rather that Governor Smith regarded Jones so highly that he "gave him a seat in the inner circle." As state architect, Jones designed three sizable projects that helped transform Albany into a modern city.

Born in 1878 in Rockland County, Jones lived most of his life in Yonkers, Washington, D.C., and New York City, where he died in 1955. He attended the Massachusetts Institute of Technology for two years but left in 1898 before graduating. By 1900 he had a small practice in New York City and spent the next decade there working for several architecture firms before becoming a partner in the firm of Hornbostel, Palmer and Jones. At that time the firm was working on its largest project, the New York State Education Building (1908–1912) and had branch offices in Albany and Pittsburgh.

In his 1911 application for membership in the American Institute of Architects, Jones reported working on the "competitive drawings" and "a full sized staff model" for the State Education Building among his projects at the firm. The application indicates that Jones was actively involved in the design of the State Education Building from the beginning, before he became a partner in 1910, up through its completion. He became a member of the AIA in 1912 and was elected a Fellow in 1927.

Today Jones is most remembered for two Art Deco skyscrapers at opposite sides of the state, in Albany and Buffalo. Jones's 1926 design for a 26-story state office building in Albany, which was to be the "tallest building between New York and Buffalo," was widely publicized. By the following year the plan was expanded to 32 stories, and what would later be named the Alfred E. Smith Building (1926–1930) began to take its final form. The Smith Building and the Buffalo City Hall were both completed in 1930 and offered the public panoramic views from open-air observation platforms.

West Capitol Park (1926–1930), also designed by Jones, stands literally at the center of his most prominent work in Albany, with the State Education Building to its north and the Alfred E. Smith Building to its west. The geometric landscape of the park, with its parallel rows of trees, curbing, and walks, was designed to create a formal visual link between the Capitol and the new state office building. A tunnel under the park links the two buildings.

Jones's third Albany project as state architect was Page, Milne, and Richardson halls (1927–1929) on the Downtown Campus of the State University. Opened for classes in September 1929, these buildings form a U-shaped grouping: Page Hall, with its neoclassical portico, urn finials, and cupola, is the focal point of the composition, set at the center of an open courtyard with

Alfred E. Smith State Office Building, Swan Street between State Street and Washington Avenue. Photograph provided by M. McCarty and G. Gold.

Milne projecting forward on the west and Richardson mirroring Milne on the east. As with all of Jones's Albany projects construction of this complex was completed after he resigned as state architect, under the supervision of his successor, William Haugaard.

1926–1930 West Capitol Park, bet. New York State Capitol and Swan St.

1927–1929 Page, Milne, and Richardson Halls, University at Albany (Downtown Campus), Washington Ave. bet. Robin St. and N. Lake Ave.

Building List

1908–1912 New York State Education Building (with Palmer and Hornbostel), Washington Ave. bet. Hawk St. and Swan St.

1926–1930 Alfred E. Smith State Office Building, Swan St. bet. State St. and Washington Ave.

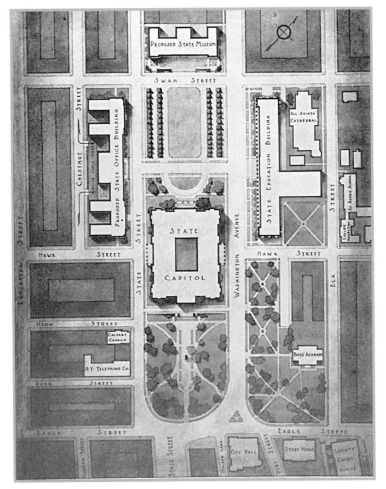

West Capitol Park, between New York State Capitol and Swan Street. New York State Library.

Henry Ives Cobb

Cornelia Brooke Gilder

Born in Brookline, Massachusetts, Henry Ives Cobb (1859–1931) was educated at the Massachusetts Institute of Technology and worked as a young man for Boston architects Peabody and Stearns. In 1882, the year of his marriage to Emma Martin Smith of New York City, he moved to Chicago after winning a competition for that city's Union Club. In partnership with Charles Frost, Cobb made his reputation in the Midwest with turreted millionaires' houses for such clients as Potter Palmer and with conspicuous civic buildings such as the Newberry Library (1887) and the Chicago Historical Society (1887). His Ownes Building of 1889 was one of the first steel-framed structures in Chicago. Later he designed as many as 18 collegiate Gothic buildings at the University of Chicago, the Chicago Opera House, and the Durant Art Institute in Lake Forest.

At the World's Columbian Exposition in Chicago in 1893, Cobb was given an opportunity to produce grand, theatrical structures, including two massive domed and glazed exhibition halls, the fisheries, and the horticultural buildings. He also created the exotic Streets of Cairo, a bazaar courtyard with a mosque entered through a Luxor-inspired portal. An enduring downtown landmark of this period of Cobb's fanciful designs is the Chicago Athletic Association (1893), which has a Venetian palazzo facade.

During a slump in construction in Chicago, Cobb moved his office to Washington, D.C., from 1896 to 1902, serving as a special U.S. government architect. He designed the League Island buildings at Annapolis and college buildings at American University. In 1899 he was commissioned to build his first bank in Albany, the Albany Savings Bank (demolished 1975), an imposing domed structure reminiscent of his work at the Columbian Exposition.

The third phase of Cobb's career was based in New York City after 1902. His best-known building in the city is the Liberty Tower (1909), a revel in Gothic terra-cotta decoration. Aside from his architectural practice, Cobb became a specialist in arbitrating building disputes and served as president of the American Arbitration Association. He also was an accomplished painter of landscapes and genre scenes.

Cobb was in his late sixties when he returned to Albany in 1926 to design his second bank. The New York State National Bank wanted to redesign its historic corner site where Philip Hooker had built the first bank, an elegant, pedimented Federal structure, in 1803. Around 1865 the structure was enlarged and heightened to four stories. Cobb was asked to make a modern, 16-story office building on this venerated site. Cobb later wrote that "the problem was a far cry from Hooker's two-story, 40-foot

building. Offhand it looked as if present-day requirements had so little to do with those of Hooker's day that Hooker's building would be completely lost in the shuffle." But the evenhanded arbitrator found a solution. Cobb skillfully reused Hooker's facade, recentering it at the base of the towering new structure and merging Hooker's motifs and materials in new arched windows and rusticated brownstone on the lower floors. Cobb died in 1931, not long after the completion of this Albany landmark.

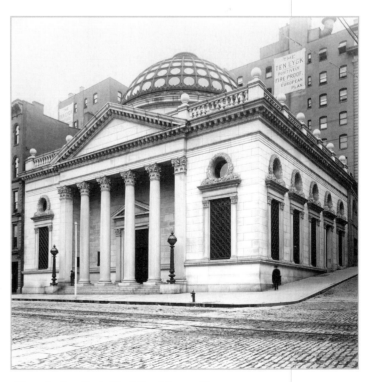

Albany Savings Bank, North Pearl Street. Albany Institute of History & Art Library.

Building List

1899   Albany Savings Bank, N. Pearl St., demolished 1975
1926   New York State National Bank (now Bank of America), 69 State St.

New York State National Bank. Photograph provided by M. McCarty and G. Gold.

New York State National Bank, 69 State Street. Albany Institute of History & Art Library.

Dennison & Hirons

Cornelia Brooke Gilder

As the 1920s roared to a close, the gifted architectural hand of the New York City firm of Dennison and Hirons summoned stylish Art Deco towers to scrape skies from Erie, Pennsylvania, to Newark, New Jersey. But none of them had the special charm of Albany's Home Savings Bank at 11 North Pearl Street, where Dennison and Hirons decorated the roofline with alternating Iroquois in feathered headdresses and helmeted Dutchman, all in gilded terra cotta.

The able English-born Frederic Charles Hirons (1882–1942) was a man who was said to draw "too easily." As a schoolboy in Boston, Hirons became a fluid, confident draftsman. He excelled during his two years at the Massachusetts Institute of Technology, won the Rotch Traveling Scholarship, and then failed in his first attempt to gain admission to the École des Beaux-Arts in 1904. He succeeded six months later and remained in Paris for the next five years, where he probably met his future professional partner, Ethan Allen Dennison (1881–1954), who also studied there.

Back in New York City, Dennison and Hirons opened a practice in 1910. The facile Hirons was the primary designer, and Dennison managed the business. They produced meticulously detailed Beaux-Arts-style buildings, such as the Chemung Canal Trust Company (1921) in Elmira, and theatrical ones, such as Childs Restaurant (1923) on Coney Island, a boardwalk eatery decorated with polychrome nautical motifs in glazed terra cotta—seahorses, galleons, and seaweed-clad mythological figures.

After 1925 Dennison and Hirons continued to use terra cotta to embellish Art Deco buildings. At the 19-story Home Savings Bank in Albany, one of their largest office buildings, Hirons's artistry went into incised floral designs at the ground-floor entrance, above fluted pilasters, over windows, and on upper levels between the vertical ribs of the soaring structure. His favored architectural sculptor, René Chambellan, of New York City, executed these designs. "The most satisfactory way," Hirons wrote in *Pencil Points*, "is to select a painter or sculptor by quality of his work—and not by competitive bids." Chambellan worked with Hirons on many other projects, including the State Bank and Trust Building (1928) in Manhattan and the Suffolk Title and Guarantee Building (1929) in Queens. Chambellan modeled a bronze plaque of Hirons on the occasion of his retirement from teaching at Columbia University in 1928.

Dennison and Hirons were active members in the Society of Beaux-Arts Architects of New York, and Hirons founded the Beaux-Arts Institute of Design, which offered exhibition space and fine-arts courses, first in an old

Home Savings Bank, 11 North Pearl Street. Albany Institute of History & Art Library.

stable and after 1928 in a handsome Art Deco building at 304–306 East Forty-fourth street designed by Hirons. At the annual Beaux-Arts ball held here, the dapper aesthete Hirons made costumes de rigueur.

In the 1930s the two practiced separately. Dennison continued to build large commercial buildings, such as the Delaware Trust Company in Wilmington (1930) and also designed a house for Alfred I. du Pont. In the 1940s he participated with Wallace K. Harrison and others in the huge Fort Greene Housing Project in Brooklyn. Hirons, with various collaborators, designed the George Rogers Clark Memorial (1930) in Vincennes, Indiana, and the Davidson County Courthouse (1935) in Nashville, Tennessee.

Building List

1927   Home Savings Bank, 11 N. Pearl St.

Home Savings Bank. Photograph provided by M. McCarty and G. Gold.

Henry L. Blatner

John I Mesick

Henry Blatner (1911–1978) was the preeminent practitioner of contemporary architectural design in Albany during the middle decades of the twentieth century. All his buildings reflected a Modernist's sensibility and concern for an economy of means. Each design was marked by innovative responses to the owner's needs. His buildings often provoked controversy in a region then more accustomed to traditional styles of building. Yet, throughout his career he attracted sympathetic clients for numerous dwellings, schools, and commercial buildings.

Born and raised in Albany, Blatner completed his undergraduate architectural education at the University of Pennsylvania in 1934. During his years at Penn the curriculum was still under the influence of the Beaux-Arts tradition—most particularly Art Deco neoclassicism. After Penn, Blatner obtained a master's degree in architecture on a graduate fellowship at the Massachusetts Institute of Technology in 1936. By that time the architectural program at MIT had largely adopted a Modernist approach to design.

Perhaps owing to the diversity of this architectural education, as well to a keen mind, Blatner's approach to the design of individual buildings was always marked by a freedom from preconceived notions of style. In undertaking each project he sought an appropriate and original solution. Moreover, his attention to detail extended to all aspects of architectural service, not only to the production of detailed drawings but to specifications and construction inspection, as well. This personal involvement continued throughout his career, even when the office staff grew to nearly 15 persons. Few architects maintain such a holistic grasp upon their work over the whole span of their career.

Throughout the late 1930s Blatner gradually established his practice in Albany. In these early years the commissions consisted largely of residences, movie theaters, and commercial buildings. His own house in Slingerlands, constructed in 1940, received national recognition with its publication in *Architectural Forum*. The interiors possessed an easy, open flow of levels and spaces reminiscent of the Bay Area style then taking root in northern California. In the adjacent Stein house (1942) he further perfected the integration of changing levels and open living spaces to create one of his finest dwellings.

With the onset of World War II Blatner closed his office and worked briefly on the design of the "big gun shop" at the Watervliet Arsenal for the Albany firm of Lux and Quackenbush. Most of the war years were spent in the Navy in Washington, D.C. The immediate post-war years

of the late 1940s and 1950s saw the realization of many of his most successful projects. Numerous houses were designed. In Albany the Brenner house (1948) on Marion Avenue and the Oppenheim house (1950s) on Manning Boulevard are two prominent projects that remain largely unaltered. The Witt house (1953) in Slingerlands was published with photos and a floor plan in *House and Home* magazine. In the early 1950s *Architectural Forum* published another of his projects, the B. T. Babbitt factory in Chicago. This cluster of industrial buildings, with an exposed-steel frame and masonry walls, further illustrated the range of his innovative design approach when he was confronted with a new building type.

In these same years Blatner commenced his extensive school-building practice. The Clarksville Elementary School came first, in 1949. Since he had never designed a school, he assured the client that he would start afresh to

Stein House, 16 Pine Hollow Road, Slingerlands, New York. Photograph provided by James A. Cohen.

discover the design best suited to their needs. Indeed, the research and creativity expended on this project launched his school-building career. An article in *Architectural Forum* praised the completed project for the innovative investigation on how best to light a classroom naturally by balancing daylight from large, north-facing windows with shielded, south-facing clerestory windows. There followed more than a dozen and a half school projects in the next 20 years. He was, perhaps, proudest of the Albany Academy for Girls (1958). This building was constructed with an exposed light-steel frame and clad with klinker bricks from the Powell and Minnock brickyard in Coeymans.

The last decade of his practice was remarkable for the great variety and scale of projects that came to his office. The most prominent of these on the Albany skyline, undoubtedly, is the South Mall Tower Apartments (1974) on South Pearl Street overlooking the arterial connector to the Empire State Plaza. He designed a library, laboratory, and lecture-hall blocks (1971) for the Albany Medical College; these were the largest, most complex structures

he had ever undertaken. Nearby, a residence hall (1968) for students at the medical college and Albany Law School was erected on Notre Dame Drive. The Jewish Community Center on Whitehall Road and the Colonie Country Club near Voorheesville also date from the early 1960s; unfortunately, both structures have been heavily altered in recent years. Three religious projects, dating from this same period, remain largely intact: the outdoor-worship court and school addition (1964) at St. John's Lutheran Church on Central Avenue, Temple Anshe Amunim (1962) in Pittsfield, Massachusetts, and the Loudonville Presbyterian Church (1961). The diversity exhibited by these late projects bears witness to a creative mind that never gave up the search for innovative solutions to the challenges each presented in its turn to the architect.

The author wishes to acknowledge the collaboration of Benjamin Mendel Jr., James A. Cohen, and Mary Blatner Valentis in the preparation of this article.

Albany Academy for Girls, 140 Academy Road.
Courtesy of the Albany Academies.

Building List

c. 1940s Elkind House, 10 Marion Ave.

c. 1940s House, 16 Marion Ave.

c. 1948 Brenner House, 84 Marion Ave.

c. 1950s Brockwell House, 233 Marion Ave., altered

c. 1950s Longe House, 229 Marion Ave., altered

c. 1950s McManus House, 223 Marion Ave., altered

c. 1950s Oppenheim House, 29 S. Manning Blvd.

c. 1953 Laventhal House, 339 S. Manning Blvd., altered

c. 1954 Albany Boys and Girls Club, 21 Delaware Ave.

c. 1954 Albany Boys and Girls Club, 520 Livingston Ave.

c. 1956 First Trust Branch Bank, 1230 Central Ave., altered

1958 Albany Academy for Girls, 140 Academy Rd., altered

c. 1958 Bennett House, Fisher Rd. and New Scotland Ave., altered

c. 1958 First Trust Branch Bank (now Key Bank), 405 Delaware Ave.

c. 1960 Office building, 194 Washington Ave., altered

c. 1961 Jewish Community Center of Albany, 340 Whitehall Rd., altered

1964 Recreation hall and school addition, St. John's Lutheran Church, 160 Central Ave.

c. 1966 Cooper Erving and Savage Law Office, 35 State St., altered

1968 Student residence, Albany Medical College and Albany Law School, 1 Notre Dame Dr.

1971 Albany Medical College, Medical Education Building and Library, 43 New Scotland Ave., altered

1974 South Mall Tower Apartments, 99 and 101 S. Pearl St.

c. 1974 Townsend Park Homes, 45 Central Ave.

South Mall Tower Apartments, 99 and 101 South Pearl Street. Photograph provided by James A. Cohen.

Albany Medical College, Medical Education Building and Library, 43 New Scotland Avenue. Courtesy of Mesick Cohen Wilson Baker Architects.

Donald Stephens

David Haviland

Donald Stephens (1918–2001) practiced architecture in Albany for 40 years, the first 10 (1946–1956) as an associate in the office of Henry Blatner and the remaining years (1956–1986) as principal, managing partner, and president of the firm Donald J. Stephens, Architects, and its successor firms. With Ronald Richard Rucinski, his associate of 29 years, Stephens designed dozens of institutional, commercial, and residential projects in Albany and the Capital Region.

Most visible are large headquarters for the New York State Teachers Retirement System, Blue Cross of Northeastern New York, and the Civil Service Employees Association. The firm designed the Daughters of Sarah Nursing Home, the Saratoga Retirement Center, the Albany Academy Field House, and the Cogswell Chemistry Laboratory on the Troy campus of Donald Stephens' alma mater, Rensselaer Polytechnic Institute. The firms' portfolio includes the U.S. Postal Service General Mail Facility in Albany and more than 60 buildings for the regional telephone company, including one for New York Telephone (1960–1969) at 9 Smith Street in Pawling, New York.

In these projects, as well as in smaller structures such as the Tri-Aird Sales Building (1967) and St. Paul's Episcopal Church (1966) in Albany, Stephens employed the rectilinear geometry, open floor plans, disciplined elevations, and careful use of concrete, masonry, and wood materials characteristic of American architecture of the 1960s and 1970s. The work is straightforward, honest, and unpretentious. One can draw a straight line from client requirements and user needs to the resulting buildings and places.

While Stephens focused his practice on institutional and commercial projects, the firm designed a number of residential projects, mostly in the suburbs—including homes for Donald Brockwell (1952), Crawford and Kay Campbell (1964), two for Jesse and Arnold Cogswell (1968, 1990), Phoebe and Matthew Bender IV (1974), and John and Dorann Zimicki—and for Albert and Katherine Fenster (1956) in Albany. The buildings are modern in form, well integrated with their sites, and generous in the use of natural light. In all of its work, the firm emphasized client communication and service as part of a "balanced approach" to architecture as art, as science, and as business.

While buildings designed by his firm dot the Capital Region landscape, Stephens's most important contributions to American architecture lie in the business aspects of architectural practice. In outlining his philosophy, he wrote, "Architecture must respond to the business aspects of the client's need, recognize the construction industry as a complex business, and relate to the constant change in the technology of construction. The profession of architecture must be practiced as a successful business to efficiently and effectively serve the client."

Over a lifetime in service to his profession, Don Stephens led a national volunteer effort to reform the way

Saint Paul's Episcopal Church, 21 Hackett Boulevard. Courtesy of Jeanne Stephens.

in which architects and their clients contracted and paid for architects' services. Stephens and his colleagues developed an approach—including a suite of national standard contract forms and management tools—that encouraged architects and their clients to select services appropriate to their projects and to base architect's fees on the actual cost of providing the selected services. This was a significant departure from the then-standard approach of basing fees on a "one size fits all" set of services and then as a percentage of the cost of constructing the resulting project. Stephens, especially, considered a fee based on construction cost as fundamentally unfair to clients (who should receive the benefit of every reasonable design effort to minimize construction costs), as well as to architects (who should not receive lesser fees as rewards for their diligent efforts to reduce construction cost).

Published by the American Institute of Architects, the contract forms that Stephens espoused to bring the straightforward, honest qualities of one architect's regional design work to the practice of all American architects. For this and other contributions, the American Institute of Architects elevated Don Stephens to the position of Fellow in 1976.

Building List

1956 Fenster House, 90 Brookline Ave.
1966 St. Paul's Episcopal Church, 21 Hackett Blvd.
1967 Albany Academy Field House, 135 Academy Rd.
1967 Tri-Aird Sales Building, Broadway at Bridge St., modified
1972 Capital Newspapers Group, 645 Albany Shaker Rd.
1973 Daughters of Sarah Nursing Home, 180 Washington Ave. Ext.
1975 Civil Service Employees Association Headquarters Building, 143 Washington Ave.
1980 U.S. Postal Service General Mail Facility, 30 Old Karner Rd.
1985 New York State Teachers Retirement System Headquarters Building, 10 Corporate Woods Dr.

New York Telephone, 9 Smith Street, Pawling, New York. Courtesy of Jeanne Stephens.

New York State Teachers Retirement System Headquarters Building, 10 Corporate Woods Drive. Courtesy of Jeanne Stephens.

Percival Goodman

Cornelia Brooke Gilder

On an open, flat site on Academy Road, Percival Goodman's Temple Beth Emeth gives the illusion of a tent pitched in the Sinai Desert: the synagogue's exterior is dominated by a huge, folded roof. Seen from certain angles, the solid brick-and-glass building is effaced, giving a view through the structure of blue sky beyond. Built in 1957, this landmark is the work of one of America's leading designers of synagogues in the post–World War II era.

Percival Goodman (1904–1989) was an architect, social theorist, and professor. Based in New York City, he influenced two generations of graduate students at the Columbia University School of Architecture between 1946 and 1971. With his brother Paul, he wrote *Communitas* (1947), a visionary city-planning text. In the 1960s Goodman became an outspoken critic of demolition-oriented urban-renewal programs, which threatened to disrupt communities and erase their history, character, and scale.

Born to an affluent and artistic Jewish family, which was convulsed into poverty by his parents' divorce, Goodman's early life was marked by instability and rebellion. He dropped out of grade school and went to work as an office boy for an architect uncle. A talented, independent youth, Goodman succeeded under the tutelage of mentors and with only a few months of formal training at Cooper Union. By the age of 21, he had made his way to Paris and the École des Beaux-Arts.

Goodman returned to New York City in 1929 and with a fellow architect from Paris, Franklin Whitman, began a successful practice designing sleek International Style department-store interiors and residences. The synagogues were to come later, when Goodman's Jewish awareness was aroused by the Holocaust. He claimed to have been "an agnostic who was converted by Hitler."

Albany's Temple Beth Emeth is one of 50 dynamic Modernist temples Goodman designed between 1947 and 1979. His synagogues can be found all over the U.S., in prosperous suburbs of Nashville, Cleveland, and Detroit and in urban settings in New York City, Providence, and Miami. Through these imaginative buildings he reinterpreted ancient Jewish traditions and employed skilled artisans for decoration, lighting, and stained glass. From 1955 to 1970 his wife, Naomi, collaborated on fabrics, furniture, and other interior-design features.

When possible, Goodman sought to use local materials to help reinforce the congregation's own history. At Albany's Beth Emeth the modern stained-glass windows by Robert Sowers integrate old windows from the congregation's downtown synagogue on Swan and Lancaster streets.

Goodman believed that designs for Jewish temples had become muddled with various hierarchical Christian plans over the years. In an article on synagogue design in *Commentary* in 1947, he wrote that "the only religious actor is the congregation." In Albany the sanctuary is wider than it is long, bringing the congregation closer to the ark and the central bimah, where members of the congregation read the scripture.

Working often with divisive building committees and opinionated benefactors, Goodman strove to elevate his synagogues beyond the community function of a country club. His admiring younger brother, Paul, described Percival's infectious ability to win over others to his own powerful vision:

> He
> Invents what people do not know they want
> But they see it come to be with surprise,
> Pleased in the end.

Temple Beth Emeth, 100 Academy Road. Photograph provided by M. McCarty and G. Gold.

Building List

1957 Temple Beth Emeth, 100 Academy Rd.

Edward Durell Stone

Hicks Stone

In 1961 the New York State University Construction Fund awarded the design of the State University of New York College at Albany to architect Edward Durell Stone. Planned on a picturesque 230-acre site, the campus was designed to accommodate 10,000 students.

Stone viewed this commission as an opportunity to address what he felt were fundamental problems in campus planning. Traditionally, most campuses grew over time, with groupings of buildings arranged around landscaped quadrangles. In Stone's view this organic, open-ended expansion harmed the natural setting, was expensive to build and operate, and created hardships for students.

To solve these problems on the Albany campus, Stone placed all of the university's academic buildings on an elevated podium. The buildings were linked by alternating open courtyards and covered colonnades. The podium and colonnades unified the buildings, giving the complex an appearance of being a single structure. Four dormitory towers with courtyards and colonnades were located near the corners of this central structure.

Stone sought to preserve the site's scenic beauty by limiting construction, producing a campus that operated economically, minimizing the automobile (which he disliked), and providing students with a campus that could be easily negotiated, even during inclement weather.

Stone was born in Fayetteville in northwest Arkansas in 1902. As an adolescent he demonstrated remarkable talent and facility as an artist. This talent took him from his modest rural beginnings to Harvard University and the Massachusetts Institute of Technology, where he won the prestigious Rotch Traveling Fellowship and toured Europe, producing an extensive portfolio of exquisite watercolors and pencil sketches of architectural monuments. He was the only American architect known to have seen Mies van der Rohe's German Pavilion at the Barcelona World's

State University of New York at Albany, 1400 Washington Avenue. Photograph provided by M. McCarty and G. Gold.

Fair. The pavilion and other Modernist architecture in the Netherlands and Great Britain strongly influenced his early work, which was starkly modern, asymmetrical, and boldly volumetric.

Upon his return to the U.S., Stone worked in the office of Raymond Hood and J. André Fouilhoux on the design of Radio City Music Hall (1932). It was on this project and on the Rockefeller Apartments (1936), which he designed while in the office of Wallace K. Harrison, that Stone established a relationship with Nelson A. Rockefeller. Some 30 years later the Rockefeller administration awarded Stone the commission for State University of New York College at Albany (renamed the State University of New York at Albany in 1962 and now known as the University at Albany, SUNY).

Stone opened his practice in the late 1930s. His reputation as one the few practicing American Modernist architects and his relationship with the Rockefeller family led to his selection as the architect for the Museum of Modern Art (1939) in New York City, his most celebrated early work.

Despite his success, Stone became disaffected with the sterility of Modernism. In the 1940s he experimented with rustic wood residences, drawing on the vernacular architecture of his boyhood. He also visited Frank Lloyd Wright at Taliesin West in Arizona. The visit was a seminal moment in Stone's development as an architect. Wright became a lifelong friend, and Stone's work began to take on many Wrightian characteristics. In particular, Wright celebrated structural columns as a decorative element by elaborating and exaggerating their components, and he favored deeply overhanging roofs with decorative openings within the cantilever. Stone employed both of these devices in his work at the State University of New York College at Albany.

Significantly, Stone differed from Wright and the Modernists in the basic organizational structure of his architecture, preferring ancient Roman ordering with strongly axial and symmetrical compositions, rather than a site-responsive and programmatically sensitive asymmetry. His wife, Maria Elena Torchio Stone, who was of Italian descent, is widely credited for encouraging his interest in ancient Roman architecture.

Stone's use of landscape elements during this period, such as colonnade-enclosed courtyards lined with rectilinear reflecting pools, landscape parterres, and fountains that are seen in SUNY Albany, have a clear precedent in the Moorish gardens of the Alhambra and Generalife in Grenada, which Stone had documented extensively in his sketches for the Rotch fellowship.

Stone's aesthetic vocabulary at SUNY Albany is a distillation of motifs borrowed from Frank Lloyd Wright, ancient Roman planning, the Moorish attitude toward integrating landscape and architectural space, and a stark geometric boldness borne out of his early Modernist work.

Building List

1961–1971   State University of New York at Albany, 1400 Washington Ave.

Wallace K. Harrison

Tara P. Monastero

Wallace Kirkman Harrison (1895–1981), born in Worcester, Massachusetts, during an era known for Beaux-Arts style, was among the most prolific Modernist architects of the twentieth century, juxtaposing traditional neoclassical, symmetrical buildings with aesthetic, asymmetrical, eclectic designs. Known for his contributions to the World's Fair Theme Center (1939), Rockefeller Center (1940), the United Nations Headquarters (1953), the Time-Life Building (1960), Lincoln Center for the Performing Arts (1962), and the Metropolitan Opera House (1965), Harrison's repertoire also includes the Gov. Nelson A. Rockefeller Empire State Plaza in Albany.

During his career Harrison collaborated with numerous partners (Harvey Wiley Corbett, Robert Perry Rodgers, Frank Helmle, William H. MacMurray, J. André Fouilhoux, Max Abramovitz), but his most unusual and fruitful partnership was with a man who called Harrison "the greatest architect of the twentieth century," Nelson A. Rockefeller. While their relationship dates back to the early 1930s during the conception, design, and construction of Rockefeller Center, Harrison and Rockefeller's affiliation includes Rockefeller's Fifth Avenue apartment (1934); the Avila Hotel in Caracas, Venezuela (1941); the Anchorage, Rockefeller's home in Maine (1941); and the Empire State Plaza (also known as the Albany Mall or South Mall).

The Justice Building (1972), Legislative Office Building (1972), Motor Vehicles Building (1972), Mayor Erastus Corning 2nd Tower (1973), Cultural Education Center (1974), Performing Arts Center (termed "The Egg," 1975), and the four agency buildings (1977) make up the South Mall. Rockefeller, who wanted to create "one of the most brilliant, beautiful, efficient, and electrifying capitals in all the world" (and who critics say had an "edifice complex"), took a direct role in its design, financing, and construction. For political reasons (and to speed up construction) firms from different parts of the state were engaged to design the structures and interiors of three buildings simultaneously. James and Meadows and Howard, of Buffalo, was selected for the Legislative Building; Sargent, Webster, Crenshaw and Folley, of Syracuse, for the Justice Building; and, Carson, Lundin and Shaw, of New York City, for the Motor Vehicles Building. Harrison's firm designed the exteriors of these buildings and also the tower and four agency buildings. The firm also produced the working drawings.

Speaking of his part in the Albany project, Harrison said, "I had a lot to do with everything Nelson didn't do with the design of the thing." Harrison, who spent time on site monthly, also contributed towards decisions involving

the Plaza's artwork (Harrison suggested that over $2.6 million be allotted). Rockefeller proposed the shape of "The Egg," imposed the use of marble (Harrison had suggested limestone), and recommended that a memorial arch be erected opposite the Capitol (where the Cultural Education Center now stands). Rockefeller also proposed changes without approval from Harrison or the Office of General Services.

The State had acquired 98.5 acres of land between the Capitol and the Executive Mansion (circa 1962) to create additional office space for state government, place emphasis on the nineteenth-century Capitol, and improve the business district, transportation, and parking. From

Empire State Plaza, Legislative Office Building.
Photograph provided by M. McCarty and G. Gold

Nelson A. Rockefeller Empire State Plaza, South Swan Street between State Street and Madison Avenue. Photograph provided by M. McCarty and G. Gold.

the beginning the South Mall (as it was called during construction) was censured for its location, the destruction of more than 3,000 houses and historic buildings, and the displacement of approximately 7,000 residents, many of whom were elderly, poor, and minorities. Mayor Erastus Corning 2nd opposed the state's ownership and financing, which cost nearly $2 billion and exceeded the $480 million estimate. Critics denounced its physical disconnection with the community (the complex sits on a platform, surrounded by a wall), its design (said to be technologically outdated by the time it was complete), and its construction (beset with labor disputes, high costs, fires, and pipe flooding) until well after the complex was completed in 1978.

Wallace K. Harrison's final monumental commission (re-named the Gov. Nelson A. Rockefeller Empire State Plaza in 1978) continues to draw government officials, workers, artists, historians, tourists, students, festivals, and ceremonies, as well as ongoing criticism and praise.

Building List

1962–1978 Nelson A. Rockefeller Empire State Plaza, S. Swan St. bet. State St. and Madison Ave.

William Brandow is a native of Albany and an associate in the firm of John G. Waite Associates, Architects in Albany, where he has worked since 1997. He holds undergraduate degrees in history and historic preservation from Roger Williams University and a master's degree in architectural conservation from the University of York in England.

T. Robins Brown is a consultant in architectural history and historic preservation who lives in Nyack, New York. She is a graduate of the University of Virginia architectural history graduate program and a former member of the board of directors of the Historic Albany Foundation.

Douglas G. Bucher is a principal with John G. Waite Associates, Architects and has spent more than 35 years investigating and restoring some of America's most important historic buildings. He is co-author of a book on Philip Hooker and of *The Marble House in Second Street*, the story of the Troy townhouse being restored by the Rensselaer County Historical Society.

Harold Colbeth, a graduate of Tufts University, worked as an architectural historian for Albany's Bureau of Historical Services. He earned a MLS from the University of Albany in 1986 and had internships with the Colonial Albany Social History Project, sponsored by the New York State Museum, and with the New York State Library.

John A. Gander, Conrad Gander's son, joined his father's and uncles' architectural practice in 1950. He died in 1984. Some records and drawings of Gander, Gander and Gander's work are housed at the Albany Institute of History and Art.

Thirty years ago *Cornelia Brooke Gilder* edited *Albany Architects*, Historic Albany Foundation's precursor of this new book. She also contributed to *Albany Architecture: A Guide to the City*. A resident of Tyringham, Massachusetts, she is co-author of two recent books on the Berkshires, *Houses of the Berkshires* and *Hawthorne's Lenox*.

David Haviland is professor of architecture emeritus, Rensselaer Polytechnic Institute. He served as dean of architecture at Rensselaer from 1980 to 1990 and as editor of the 1986 and 1994 editions of *The Architect's Handbook of Professional Practice*, published by the American Institute of Architects.

William J. Higgins is a principal in Higgins Quasebarth & Partners, a historic preservation consulting firm in New York City founded in 1983. He is a native of Troy, New York, and holds a master's degree in historic preservation from Columbia University.

Andrea J. Lazarski has worked for the State Commission on the Restoration of the Capitol since 1988. She was the administrator of the Kansas City, Missouri, Landmarks Commission and was the preservation planner for the City of Ithaca, New York. She has served on numerous not-for-profit boards and was president of Historic Albany Foundation.

John I Mesick, currently a principal in the firm of Mesick Cohen Wilson Baker Architects, LLP, began his practice in Albany in partnership with Henry Blatner and Benjamin Mendel Jr. in 1965. During the intervening decades he has been largely engaged in the preservation of historic sites, including Henry Hobson Richardson's Senate and Executive Chambers in the Capitol.

Tara P. Monastero is co-editor of *TechKnowledgies: New Imaginaries in the Humanities, Arts, and TechnoSciences* and *13th Moon: A Feminist Literary Magazine*, Volume XVIII. She earned her bachelor's degree in English at Mount Saint Mary College in Newburgh, New York, and master's degrees in English and women's studies at the University at Albany.

Jessica Fisher Neidl is a native of Albany, New York, and is a freelance writer, with an avid interest in local history and architecture. She holds a master's degree in classics and a bachelor's degree in English from the University at Albany. Her family has called Albany home for more than 150 years.

Willow Partington is on the faculty of Hudson Valley Community College in Troy, where she has taught the history of art, poetry, public speaking, writing, theatre, and Native American literature. She lives in southern Washington County, New York.

Kenneth G. Reynolds Jr., grandnephew of Marcus T. Reynolds, was an architect in the office of Lux and Quackenbush, the successor firm to the office of Marcus Reynolds. The office maintained Marcus Reynolds's original drawings from 1895, which are now in the collection of the Albany Institute of History and Art. Kenneth Reynolds's essay was augmented with information from E. J. Johnson's study, *Style Follows Function: Architecture of Marcus T. Reynolds*.

Norman S. Rice is director emeritus of the Albany Institute of History and Art and has been chairman of the Historic Resources Commission for the City of Albany since 1981. He served as the Albany city historian from 1966 to 1987.

Lewis C. Rubenstein, a graduate of the Winterthur Program in American Cultural History, was an early opponent of ill-conceived urban renewal and road-building projects. Starting as director-curator of a small historical society in Newburyport, Massachusetts, and continuing in several New York State government posts, he served the cause of historic preservation for 32 years.

Hicks Stone, a son of Edward Durell Stone, is an architect in New York City. His firm, Stone Architecture, designs luxury private residences and compelling public spaces throughout North America. He is currently writing a biography of his father and a monograph of his work entitled *Edward Durell Stone: Man and Architect* for Rizzoli International Publications.

Erin M. Tobin works for the Preservation League of New York State as regional director of technical and grant programs, serving as the primary field services staff for Eastern New York, New York City, and Long Island. She is also involved with the Northeast Chapter of the Association for Preservation Technology and the Recent Past Preservation Network.

Diana S. Waite, president of Mount Ida Press, was the editor of *Albany Architecture: A Guide to the City* and since 1991 has edited the *APT Bulletin: The Journal of Preservation Technology*. She has written histories for the New York Yacht Club, the Fort Orange Club, and the University of Virginia.

Walter Richard Wheeler is senior architectural historian for Hartgen Archeological Associates, Inc., and serves on the board of the Albany County Historical Association. He has prepared a monograph on Henry Rector's work and is currently writing a book on the vernacular architecture of the upper Hudson Valley for SUNY Press.

Supplemental Credits

Poem on page 70 is from Kimberly J. Elman and Angela Giral, eds., *Percival Goodman, Architect, Planner, Teacher, Painter* (New York: Wallach Art Gallery, Columbia University, 2001), 109.

Page 3, top. St. Paul's Church, corner of South Ferry and Dallius Sts., Albany, N.Y., unidentified photographer, not dated, source of original print unknown, No. 1993.010.3877.2P. Morris Gerber Photograph Collection, Albany Institute of History & Art Library.

Page 5. North Pearl Street Baptist Church, northwest corner of North Pearl St. and Maiden La., Albany, N.Y., unidentified photographer, c. 1830-1850, No. 1993.010.3890.2P. Morris Gerber Photograph Collection, Albany Institute of History & Art Library.

Page 7. "Trinity Episcopal Church" from Joel Munsell, Munsell's Annals of Albany, vol. 3 (Albany, N.Y.: 1850), 265. Albany Institute of History & Art Library, 974.743.

Page 8. Delavan House, northeast corner of Broadway and Steuben St., Albany, N.Y., unidentified photographer, not dated, but prior to 1894, No. 1993.010.6432P. Morris Gerber Photograph Collection, Albany Institute of History & Art Library.

Page 12, interior, Saint Joseph's Roman Catholic Church, Albany, N.Y. Robert N. Dennis Collection of Stereoscopic Views, Miriam and Ira D. Wallach Division of Art, Prints and Photographs, The New York Public Library, Astor, Lenox and Tilden Foundations.

Page 15, top. Church of the Holy Innocents, 271 North Pearl St., Albany, N.Y., unidentified photographer, not dated, Mo. 1993.010.3903P. Morris Gerber Collection, Albany Institute of History & Art Library.

Page 25. Thomas Fuller, design for the New York State Capitol. *Harper's Weekly*, October 9, 1869. Courtesy of the New York State Commission on the Restoration of the Capitol.

Page 26, top. Leopold Eidlitz, design for New York State Capitol. *American Architect and Building News*, April 15, 1876. Courtesy of the New York State Commission on the Restoration of the Capitol.

Page 35, top. Albany Institute of History & Art, 125 Washington Ave., Albany, N.Y., unidentified photographer, c. 1930, No. 1793. Main Photograph Collection, Albany Institute of History & Art.

Page 37. Exterior of First Presbyterian Church of Albany, State and Willet Sts., Albany, N.Y., possibly Stephen Schreiber, photographer, not dated, No. 1993.010.3931.1P. Morris Gerber Photograph Collection, Albany Institute of History & Art Library.

Page 39, top right. Proposed All Saints Cathedral, Albany, N.Y., dedicated 1886, unidentified artist, likely the firm of Robert W. Gibson, Architect, after 1886, Pkg, XIII; #38g. Albany Institute of History & Art.

Page 39, top left. The Lodge at Albany Rural Cemetery, from George Howell and Jonathon Tenney, *History of Albany County*, vol. 2, City of Albany (New York: W. W. Munsell and Co., Publishers, 1886), 675. Albany Institute of History & Art Library, 974.742.

Page 40. Steamer No. 1 Firehouse, Washington and Western Aves., Albany, N.Y., unidentified photographer, c. 1900. Main Photograph Collection, 2-41 g, Albany Institute of History & Art.

Page 45. Interior of Union Station, 575 Broadway, Albany, N.Y., unidentified photographer, c. 1930-1940, No. 1993.010.9636P. Morris Gerber Collection, Albany Institute of History & Art.

Page 55, left. Hudson River Day Line Ticket Office, W. Hunter Van Guysling, watercolor on paper, 1907. Gift of Alfred Van Santvoort Olcott, 1949.51.2. Albany Institute of History & Art.

Page 56. Albany County Courthouse, Eagle and Columbia Sts., Albany, N.Y., unidentified photographer, undated, No. 1993.010.4749P. Morris Gerber Collection, Albany Institute of History & Art.

Page 58. Post Office Courtroom, Broadway, unidentified artist, 1931-1936, Gander, Gander and Gander Papers, 1916-1969, HE 80-03, Box 1, Folder 3. Albany Institute of History & Art Library.

Page 61. Albany Saving Bank, North Pearl St. at Maiden La., c. 1910. Hinkleman Photography Collection, Albany Institute of History & Art.

Page 62, left. New York State National Bank, 69 State St. (lower left photo [N.E. Corner]), J. A. Glenn, Albany, N.Y., not dated, No. 1993.010.2048.1P. Morris Gerber Photograph Collection, Albany Institute of History & Art Library.

Page 63. Home Savings Bank, 11 North Pearl St., Albany, N.Y., possibly Stephen Schreiber, Jr. not dated, No. 1993.010.3002P. Morris Gerber Collection, Albany Institute of History & Art Library.